AFTER
DIVORCE

Hope for Catholics

SUSAN K. ROWLAND

ST. ANTHONY MESSENGER PRESS
Cincinnati, Ohio

LIBRARY OF CONGRESS CATALOGING-IN-PUBLICATION DATA
Rowland, Susan K.
Healing after divorce : hope for Catholics / Susan K. Rowland.
p. cm.
Includes bibliographical references (p.   ).
ISBN 097-8867169805 (pbk. : alk. paper)
1. Divorce--Religious aspects--Catholic Church. 2. Divorced people--Religious life. I. Title.
BX2254.R69 2010
248.8'6--dc22
2010020493

ISBN 978-0-86716-980-5

Published by St. Anthony Messenger Press
28 W. Liberty St.
Cincinnati, OH 45202
www.AmericanCatholic.org
www.SAMPBooks.org

Printed in the United States of America.

Printed on acid-free paper.

10 11 12 13 14 5 4 3 2 1

To my family and friends
who helped me through the transition, especially:
My mother, Ida Bielecki
My brother, Thom Spring
Marilyn Collins
Kathy and Jim Scarnecchia
Elaine Polomsky Soos
Dr. Blythe Robinson
Dr. Joseph Torma
and
Mother Nadine Brown and the
Intercessors of the Lamb Community,
who gave me a place of refuge
when I needed it most.

contents

acknowledgments

My thanks, again, to Lisa Biedenbach and the staff at St. Anthony Messenger Press for their support over the years and for the opportunity to publish another book together. It's good to be part of the family!

My heartfelt thanks also go to:

Attorney James L. Messenger of Youngstown, Ohio, for taking the time out of a busy practice to answer my many questions.

Father Jack Spaulding, pastor of St. Timothy Catholic Church in Mesa, Arizona, whose talks on marriage clarified many of my own issues.

Julie and Frank LaBoda, International Coordinating Team of Retrouvaille, for their commitment to healing troubled marriages and willingness to answer my questions.

Kass, Kim, Mary, Martin, and Paul, who opened their hearts and shared their stories.

Terry Hershey for his friendship, encouragement, and constant reminders of what is important in this life.

My sisters at the Women's Fellowship of St. Timothy Parish, who have supported me with prayers and hugs throughout the writing of this book.

introduction

My condolences to you who have picked up this book because you are recently divorced. I have been there—watching my life fall apart, seeing my dreams end, knowing my future would not be remotely what I imagined. Yet, there is hope in all this. God loves us. God's love is not diminished or changed one iota when we get divorced. God is not disappointed in us, nor thinks less of us. If we allow it, God will be close at this time, guiding us through the rough waters to a peaceful, calm, holy place.

When my marriage was ending and I knew I would be divorced soon, I reacted like a seriously injured person overhearing talk about amputation. I was panic-stricken, nervous, fearful, unsure of myself. Divorce is, in fact, the amputation of a relationship. The healing will take years. Some of us never seem to heal. That is why I wrote this book: to help bring about healing and health for all of us who are divorced. The divorced are members of the body of Christ, just as the married and single are. Divorce is difficult and those experiencing it need to be ministered to, just as the sick, the dying, and the impoverished do.

Who am I? I am a survivor of divorce after being married over thirty years. I have not only survived, but I have healed many hurts and relieved myself of the heavy baggage I brought into my marriage. I am more whole and happy than ever before. Life is good today. In fact, life is a miracle.

Ten years ago, when my life crashed down around me, I thought I would never feel this way. But God is good and faithful, especially to those who are "afflicted," "storm-tossed," and "not comforted" (Isaiah 54:11).

For those of you going through or having gone through the trauma of divorce, this is what God promises us:

...their life shall become like a watered garden,
and they shall never languish again.

...

I will turn their mourning into joy,
I will comfort them, and give them gladness for sorrow.
(Jeremiah 31:12, 13)

part one

THE

HOUSE

OF

CARDS

Keep your heart with all vigilance,
for from it flow the springs of life.
—Proverbs 4:23

chapter one

LIVING WITHOUT LOVE

Coming out of denial is frightening because we have no
clear understanding of where the path will lead.
—Barbara Leahy Shlemon,
Healing the Wounds of Divorce: A Spiritual Guide to Recovery[1]

In January of 2000, my husband announced, "We need to have a talk."
I was shocked by what he had to say, although if I am honest with
myself it didn't surprise me that much. He wanted out of our marriage.
In a reversal of our usual conversations, he talked and I listened. I
made a few observations, but mostly I sat in stunned silence. After a
while, I stomped out of the room, fleeing to my usual place of refuge:
the bathroom.

Wide-eyed and panicky, I gaped at my reflection in the mirror and
thought, "What now?" Part of me knew I had been waiting for this day,
seeing its approach, trying with every fiber of my being to prevent it.

Prayer came later. "How could you?" I asked God. "I asked you to help
me make my marriage better, and this is your answer? Help me. I can't
do this." Lots of words came. Panic prayers. Weeping prayers. Pleading,
don't-let-this-happen prayers. And finally, after many months of prayer,
I found peace.

It would be a while before I understood God wasn't the one breaking
up our marriage. It was broken already. Truthfully, it hadn't been much

of a marriage, and God was setting me free from an unworkable, impossible relationship.

God's timing is always perfect. My husband's announcement took place at the beginning of the Jubilee Year, 2000. The Scripture theme for that Holy Year was Jesus' "Mission Statement" of Luke 3:18, part of which promises: "[God] has sent me to proclaim release to the captives …to let the oppressed go free" (Luke 4:18).

The last thing I wanted the evening my husband made his announcement was to be "set free."

Denial: "The Hippo in the Living Room"

Ours was a long marriage. I was convinced that longevity meant health. There were problems, but my attitude was, "If we're still together, we must be OK. Every marriage has problems. The important thing is to stick together and tough it out."

If my husband and I had a fight, I would tiptoe around until the bad feelings and tension dissipated—or I pushed them safely below the surface. If there was trouble between one of our sons and their dad, it was my job to be the peacemaker. If my husband said something disrespectful to me, I kept my mouth shut and swallowed my hurt. Keeping the peace, keeping things on an even keel, going on as though nothing had happened—that was my formula.

Author Barbara Leahy Shlemon calls this "hippopotamus in the living room" syndrome:

> In this scenario the hippo has obviously established residency in the home but no one is willing to admit its existence. Instead the family members walk around it, decorate it, put slip covers over it, build on another room to accommodate it, but never, ever do they say to one another, "There's a hippo in the living room."[2]

This "marital hippo" has a name: *denial*. Denial takes many forms and tells many lies:

"Every marriage has problems."

"It isn't as bad as you're making out."

"It's all your imagination."

"Just calm down, and everything will be all right."

"This, too, shall pass."

God does not allow us to live long in our denial, in our false lives. In fact, Jesus' main purpose in coming to this world and dying for us was to set us free. God will not be inactive while we are enslaving ourselves, denying reality.

What Does God Think About Divorce?

For most of my marriage, I held to a firm conviction that good people don't get divorced. This conviction became a problem when my marriage was ending. The thought that I was soon to be divorced was powerful enough to send me into anxiety attacks. Nearly daily attacks of the shakes caused some serious physical health problems later.

It took two years between that talk in January of 2000 and the day we appeared in court for our final divorce hearing. In that time, I met regularly with a Christian psychologist and a spiritual director. I joined a divorce support group, wept on numerous friends' shoulders, and spent a lot of time in prayer. When I emerged from court in February of 2002, newly divorced, I was not entirely free in my spirit. But I had learned a great deal about God and about marriage and divorce.

I understand now that good people do get divorced. And God can support that decision.

I know beyond doubt that God loves me and loves all of us, divorced or married, widowed or single. Divorce does not change God's love for me or you. God has every hope for us. God knows that we are works in progress.

I recognize that not every married couple is "joined by God." Human effort cannot build a healthy marriage. One spouse in a marriage cannot "save" the marriage if the other is not committed. Only two people who are humbly dependent on God can possibly commit themselves to a covenant of godly love. When I married at nineteen, I did not have the commitment to God nor the ability to love needed to enter into a Christian marriage, a sacred covenant of love—and neither did my husband. Since we never sought counseling or any mature help from outside, our marriage turned into a disaster.

If you are starting on the long road out of denial and into a new freedom, if you are on the road to divorce or have already been divorced, I can promise you one thing: God is with you.

When my divorce journey began, part of me believed that I was disappointing God, that my standing with God would now change. "I know God loves me, but...." I would think. But what? "God will love me, but not as much"? There are no "buts" regarding God's love.

God's love for us, especially us broken-hearted divorced, is infinitely tender and loving. God cannot help but love us, for God *is* love. God cannot be disappointed in us, for that would imply that God had no idea of the future and had expectations of us that we did not fulfill.

God knows all the ins and outs of relationships. God knows all the issues we have hidden deep down (even from ourselves) which made us choose the mate we chose. God has seen all our efforts to make it work. God has seen all the denial. God knows our hearts thoroughly. And God loves us, plain and simple, no "buts."

And God often sets us free from marriages that are false, sick, and unworkable.

The spiritual work of a healthily married couple is to discover in their self-giving that same love that God always pours out.

For those of us who are divorced or are about to be, that discovery of God's love in a marriage partner is no longer open to us. The spiritual work that we are called to do now is to heal from our disappointment in human love, the failure of that relationship, the broken heart. Then we can move on to discover God's love, the only love which will never fail us.

For Reflection

1. What has your attitude been about divorce over the years? Did you, too, believe that good people don't get divorced?

_____

_____

_____

_____

_____

2. In what ways has denial been a part of your marriage?

_____

_____

_____

_____

_____

3. Have you had fears or doubts about God's love for you when you considered divorce?

_____

_____

_____

_____

_____

4. In what ways have you seen God's presence, care, and tough love during the worst times in your marriage and divorce?

_____

_____

_____

_____

_____

5. Take some time to write your own thoughts.

chapter two

LOOKING AT THE MARRIAGE COVENANT

From the very beginning the Church has seen in the mutual love of
married Christians a glimpse of the love of God. Faithfulness in
Christian marriage gives a hint of God's faithfulness to us as a people.
—Seán Wales, *Catholics and Divorce:
Finding Help and Healing Within the Church*[1]

This is a book about divorce, but we need to start with marriage. What
does God intend marriage to be? Is it supposed to be permanent? Is it a
legal contract or a solemn, holy covenant? Can it be put aside under any
and all circumstances?

Look at the quote above by Seán Wales. We human beings, infected
with sin and selfishness, can barely grasp God's infinite love in this life.
The mutual self-giving of a healthily married couple is only a shadow of
God's selfless, eternal, vast, and boundless love. But we, who are spiritual babes, must start somewhere. So we start with our relationships.
Most of us start with loving parents (we hope), siblings, and good
friends who prepare us to love. Eventually we meet and fall in love with
our spouses. For some of us children come along and further our amazing experience with earthly love. We spend our lifetimes learning to love
God by loving all these people in our lives, who at once can thrill and
frustrate us, and who have more power than anyone on earth to hurt us.
Anytime we love someone we run the risk of exposing ourselves to hurt.

And yes, even our spouses, the people we chose to spend our lives with, have the power to hurt us too.

Christian Marriage

What does Christianity teach and believe about marriage? While specific rules and regulations may differ (slightly), every Christian denomination views marriage as a permanent and holy covenant, reflecting the covenant God has made to love and take care of us. Divorce is seen as a distressing cultural phenomenon, something to be avoided if at all possible. Leaders of churches are urged to support and care for married couples and counsel those whose marriages are failing or have failed. I found no Christian denomination, even the supposed liberal ones, that had a laissez-faire attitude about divorce. All were distressed about the divorce rate and seeking ways to help couples succeed in the ideal of Christian marriage. Our society's denigration of marriage has been the chief topic of every denomination's leadership meetings for decades.

Why Is Christian Marriage So Difficult?

We human beings, at our worst, tend to be selfish and overly independent. This is not healthy. This is a sinful autonomy and isolation from God and one another. This independence becomes a problem when two people try to live together in the covenant of marriage. Marriage takes effort, tune-ups, and ongoing commitment if it is going to work. And that effort must be made by both parties.

Marriage is the training program into which the vast majority of human beings throughout history have entered to learn about God's love and purpose. This training program tests our patience, our kindness, and selflessness—or our ability to give without counting the cost. As each partner in a healthy marriage grows in love of the other spouse, their love for God grows, whether they are aware of it or not.

The *Catechism of the Catholic Church (CCC)* expresses this idea perfectly: "…marriage helps to overcome self-absorption, egoism, pursuit of one's own pleasure, and to open oneself to the other, to mutual aid and to self-giving."[2] It also states:

> Every man experiences evil around him and within himself. This experience makes itself felt in the relationships between man and woman. Their union has always been threatened by discord, a spirit of domination, infidelity, jealousy, and conflicts that can escalate into hatred and separation. This disorder can manifest itself more or less acutely, and can be more or less overcome according to the circumstances of cultures, eras, and individuals, but it does seem to have a universal character.[3]

Why has marriage always been hard? We humans have within us and in our society certain traits. We Christians call these traits "sin." Our sin makes *any* relationship difficult, much less the intense and permanent one that we call marriage.

Ultimately, marriage is a vocation, a calling by God to live out a form of service for our spouse, our children, and our society for the rest of our lives. We cannot know or prepare for everything that is going to happen over a lifetime together. We should have at least a fledgling relationship with God and be trusting God to help us carry out this commitment. Face it: The marriage vows are audacious and arrogant. We are promising not only to love and be faithful to this person for the rest of our lives, but we agree that even sickness and poverty may be included in the mix. None of us should make marital vows without a *soupçon* of humility and dependence on God. More important, God must be the one who has called us to make the marital commitment, before we even consider joining ourselves with another.

Where does that leave Christians who had every intention of living up to the covenant, but who are now divorced or about to be?

Jesus said "what God has joined together, let no one separate" (Mark 10:9). This can make a divorced Christian feel terrible guilt. But, let's be honest. *Did* God join us together, or did we join ourselves, with no real intention of seeking God's will about the marriage partner we chose?

Serving God as Jesus Did: Single

If marriage is a great idea and a wonderful training ground for learning God's love and holiness, it is not the only path we can choose. Jesus was single. Did you ever wonder why?

If marriage were the only way to learn about God, Jesus would have married. He would have shown us by example that aspect of living in God. But he didn't. Think about this: Jesus was baptized by John the Baptist, something the sinless Son of God did not have to do for his own benefit. He did that to show us by example that baptism is essential to the Christian life. But Jesus did not get married.

Marriage is not necessary to learn about the love of God. It is one way. It is a common way, but not the only way. A person who has always been single or is now divorced or widowed is not a second-class citizen of the kingdom. Marriage does have lessons to teach, but so does the single life. In fact, Saint Paul, single himself, was rather prejudiced toward the single life, feeling that it offered the Christian a unique opportunity to grow in holiness and to serve God more completely (see 1 Corinthians, chapter seven, verses 7–8 and 32–35).

And remember, when we leave this world, we each immediately become single again. There is no marriage in heaven.

For Reflection

1. What was your belief about the institution of marriage when you got married? Was it simply a civil/legal arrangement? Or was it a solemn covenant before God?

_____

_____

_____

_____

_____

_____

2. How did sin affect your married life? What selfishness can you now see in yourself that contributed to the marriage's failure?

_____

_____

_____

_____

_____

3. Did God "join you together" when you married? Or did you and your spouse do the joining with little or no consideration for God's will?

_____

_____

_____

_____

_____

4. Have you believed that marriage is the best way to live the Christian life? Are you all right being single and serving God in that capacity, as Jesus did?

_____

_____

_____

_____

_____

5. Take some time to write your own thoughts.

_____

_____

_____

_____

_____

chapter three

TESTING YOUR
MARRIAGE'S HEALTH

...a good marriage is both a mystery and a miracle.
It depends less on finding the right partner
than being the right partner.
—Rowland Croucher[1]

"You seemed like such a happy couple."

This was one of the more painful and *true* comments several people made to me after my divorce. It was painful because we had been married so long, and I did so badly want us to be the happy couple we appeared to be in public. But the comment was *true* because we only seemed happy—because no one had any idea what was going on below the surface or behind closed doors. Going to church together, leading the Cub Scout pack together, going to family gatherings, parent-teacher conferences, a neighbor's graduation party, did not mean we were happy or healthy. Public appearances do not a happy couple make. The only two people who know what is going on in a marriage are the two people living it. No one from the outside looking in can guess whether a couple is happy, on the brink of divorce, or somewhere in between.

What are the signs of a healthy, happy marriage? And what signs mean a marriage is in trouble? I have talked to lawyers, marriage counselors, clergy, and the folks at Retrouvaille to compile the lists below.[2]

Healthy Marriage Traits

• *Ongoing commitment and personal growth.* Each partner is vested in the marriage and feels a deep obligation to the other. Each is growing spiritually and is actively encouraging the other to grow. Regular marital check-ups will be part of a healthy marriage. Couples face different issues at different ages. Each stage of life calls for new growth, compromises, and levels of patience.

• *A relationship with God as the third partner in the marriage.* Healthy couples depend on God, who alone can help us keep our promises. We cannot do this alone. Mere human love is not equal to the task of a lifelong, Christian commitment.

• *Truth, honesty, and transparency.* Each spouse feels that he or she can share anything. Neither feels he or she must hide feelings, opinions, or eccentricities. Each feels safe with the other, especially safe to make mistakes and to be human.

• *Shared activities balanced with individual activities.* Healthy married couples do not need to share every waking moment or activity together. They have plenty of shared interests and friends, and they have individual interests and friends as well.

• *Intimacy.* Not only sex, but touching, hugging, back rubs, lying in each other's arms, kissing, welcoming each other home at the end of the day.

• *Hospitality.* A marriage partnership is the creation of a new family unit and a new social unit. Hospitality is one mark of a healthy relationship in which family, friends, neighbors, and children are welcomed into the couple's life.

• *Communication.* Effective, regular communication on a deep, personal level is basic to a healthy marriage. Discussion, compromise, and cooperation will be needed throughout married life. Couples should not stop talking, no matter how long married or how well they know each other.

Finances, gender roles, responsibilities, careers, kids, hopes, and dreams will always be issues.

• *Conflict resolution.* Arguments are inevitable in any relationship. Healthy couples know how to fight and how to forgive. They express themselves respectfully and use "me" messages instead of "you" accusations. They know they can disagree and still feel loved, respected, and safe when a fight is over.

• *Forgiveness.* A good marriage includes two good forgivers. A lifetime of marriage between two imperfect people is going to require much forgiveness. Forgiveness means letting things go completely, never bringing them up again. It is proof that God is present in the relationship.

• *Sense of humor.* A lifelong marital commitment is going to be grim if there is no laughter or play. Humor helps us take ourselves less seriously. It smoothes over the rough spots. Regular laughter and shared family jokes are the glue that holds relationships together and makes them fun.

Unhealthy Marriage Traits
• *Indifference.* An indifferent marriage is not a Christian marriage. When one partner doesn't care about what the other partner is doing, it is the ultimate form of selfishness and can be the death of a healthy marriage.

• *God is not part of the marriage.* One or both spouses have no relationship with God and no desire for that relationship. What most Christians call "lack of conversion" to Jesus means that a marital partner will be unable to give genuine love or forgiveness to the other. Lacking God's brand of divine love leaves a marriage open to whatever the culture, world, flesh, and devil, can do to it.

• *Stagnation.* The couple no longer expresses love or concern for one another. They have fallen into a rut of work, television, silence, or social activities. There is no spiritual growth, no discussion, no intimacy. They live together under one roof, maybe like brother and sister, maybe with occasional sex, but they do not share a common life. Each has friends, activities, and work that keep them busy. And they do not look forward to going home to the other partner at the end of the day.

• *Lack of communication.* The couple cannot talk about the things that matter to them: hopes, dreams, faith, feelings, anything intimate or challenging. They cannot negotiate or argue without descending into insults, accusations, nasty words, put-downs, bringing up past injuries, or disrespecting one another.

• *Isolation.* Neither spouse is allowed to have his or her own friends or interests outside the marriage because it is seen as disloyal or a betrayal. Neither partner has friends with whom they share confidences. We need more than the person we married to feel complete. Jealous partners who share an "us-against-the-world" mentality are unhealthy people, and their marriage is more likely to fail.

• *Control of all finances by one spouse.* Each partner should have some independent funds for which he or she does not have to account to the other. Otherwise, the controlled partner will feel like a child, always forced to ask for pocket money.

• *Lack of intimacy.* While intimacy within a marriage includes sex, it is not limited to sexual acts alone. When a couple no longer wants to touch one another, such as giving back rubs or hugging, kissing, or holding each other, this is a sign there is trouble. Sex may be the last form of intimacy to go, but it will go eventually if there is no other physical touch happening.

• *Lack of forgiveness.* No argument or mistake is ever forgotten or forgiven. No discussion can be had and no problem brought up by the spouse without a litany of past failures and "you always" accusations. No apology is enough. Every incident is stored away for future ammunition.

• *Mental and emotional problems.* These include substance abuse, gambling and pornography/sexual addictions, and mental illnesses such as depression, schizophrenia, and obsessive-compulsive disorders. Workaholism and a tendency to want to control others are also emotional problems. Each of these problems must be addressed by professional counseling and constant vigilance, especially by the addicted or mentally ill person.

Freely and Without Reservation?

In most marriage ceremonies, religious or secular, the priest, minister, or judge asks the couple a simple question before going on to the marriage vows. It is something like this: "Have you come here freely and without reservation?" The difference between healthy marriages and unhealthy marriages is summed up in these words: *Freely and without reservation.*

Healthy marriages not only begin "without reservation," but they continue so throughout the years. Each partner knows the other well enough to know that he or she is committed to God and to the relationship, that the other looks upon marriage as a lifelong covenant and is ready and willing to do whatever is necessary to make it work.

Good marriages are free. Each partner feels free to be him- or herself. Each trusts the other person with their feelings, secrets, hurts, dreams, and hopes. Neither feels coerced or controlled, actively or passively. Each feels that any topic, any problem, any issue can be brought up and will be discussed in a mature way. Even an out-and-out argument will not lead to destruction of that trust, for each knows the other's love is strong and faithful.

For Reflection

1. While reading this chapter, what jumped out at you as the chief problem during your marriage?

_____

_____

_____

2. What have you learned most about yourself in the divorce process? What would you have done differently in your marriage? How can you turn your negative qualities into positive ones?

_____

_____

_____

_____

_____

3. Take some time to write your own thoughts.

_____

_____

_____

_____

_____

_____

_____

_____

_____

_____

_____

_____

_____

_____

_____

_____

_____

_____

_____

_____

chapter four

HEARING FROM GOD AND KNOWING WHEN IT'S OVER

> There are times in life when God seems to be absent, but when he
> reveals himself…the experience is not of an absent God returning but
> of an always present and loving God disclosing himself again.
> —Andrew M. Greeley, *When Life Hurts:*
> *Healing Themes from the Gospels*[1]

It had almost been a year since my husband first announced he wanted a divorce. We had been through a Retrouvaille weekend (for more information on this program designed to help married couples in trouble visit http://www.retrouvaille.org). We attended several follow-up sessions. I was also seeing a counselor. In spite of all efforts, things got worse. He had said several times that he was indifferent to me and to our marriage and wanted it to be over. I had to make a decision: Either get a divorce or continue pretending by living in a marriage that was not a marriage.

I called a friend—my spiritual mother—who is the head of a religious community in Nebraska. When I told her what was going on, her first words were, "You have to hear from God before you make a decision. Come. Come and stay with us." I made arrangements to stay with my friend and her community for two weeks.

Hearing From God

How do we hear from God? Over the years, I have learned to tell when God is speaking to me, to hear God's voice welling up within me. But how could I trust that voice when I was in such dire straits emotionally? How would I know God was speaking to me through all the drama and confusion?

The uncertainty, self-doubt, and stress of watching your marriage deteriorate are a tough atmosphere for hearing from God. But God does, indeed, come to us and speak during these times. Scripture, friends, a wise spiritual director, your own journals, and that "small, still voice" that wells up from within—that voice you know cannot possibly be your own—steer you into the place where you know what decision to make.

My first week at the retreat center included quiet time, good meals, and worship with the community. I spent a lot of time in the chapel, took long walks, and enjoyed the countryside. By the end of that first week, my emotions were calmer and my mind clearer. Then I entered into an eight-day silent retreat. The only conversations I had were with a wise retreat director and with God. My retreat director knew nothing about me or my marriage. Yet her guidance, the Scripture passages she chose, and her feedback to my journal entries was so right and true, I knew it was coming from God. Even today, a decade later, every word in my retreat journal rings true. I know beyond doubt that I heard from God very clearly.

What about you? What should you do if you have come to this point, if you have tried everything you know to do, and your marriage seems over?

You must find ways of pulling away from your situation and getting alone with God. You need clear answers from God and the quiet in which to receive them.

A retreat away from home with a spiritual director is a good idea, if you can arrange it. If that is not possible, go to a friend's or relative's home for a week or two of rest and quiet. You can also check into a nearby hotel or bed-and-breakfast for a few days.

You will also need a place in your home where you can go to be alone and quiet, a place where your spouse and children are not allowed to intrude. If you do go on a retreat, you have to come home eventually. You need to have your own space to rest, pray, be quiet, journal, and think.

God, You, and Divorce

As you are making your decision, you need to remember that God loves you completely and perfectly. God's love for you will not change, no matter what decision you make. God does not bless indifferent, dead, or abusive relationships.

God knows all about you and all about your marriage. God knew long before you did what was wrong, how wrong it was, what it was doing to you, and where it was going.

Often, we finally see how awful things are because God engineered a crisis which made us wake up and see reality. Denial is the hallmark of the unhealthy marriage. We do not see because we do not want to see. But God is not into denial. God is very fond of reality. Remember Jesus' words in John 8:32: "You will know the truth, and the truth will make you free."

God loves good marriages. But when truth, honesty, and simple decency are gone, when we make choices that harm each other, when our whole life together becomes a mockery of true marriage, God reserves the right to shake things up, to see if there is anything there to save.

You need to seek God's wisdom about your particular situation. You need to do what Jesus said: "Ask, and it will be given to you; search, and you will find; knock, and the door will be opened for you" (Matthew 7:7). Your answer will not be long in coming.

Some Signs That It's Over

Keeping in mind that you must seek God's guidance, here are some general signs that a marriage is over:

• *Things have been said that can never be unsaid that change the very truth of your marriage covenant.* I do not mean words said in anger. I mean basic statements along the lines of, "I don't love you, and I don't think I ever have." Or, "I did not marry you because I loved you. I married you because _____." There are any number of ways to fill in that blank: "I was hiding that I am gay." "I wanted to get away from my parents." "I was going to a war zone and wanted to make sure you were waiting for me." "My biological clock was ticking, and you came along."

• *You have suffering, and are at the end of your rope.* Barring a miracle from God, there is nothing more you can do. And you have waited a long time for the miracle, but your spouse doesn't seem to want it. This is especially true when adultery, addictions, and abuse are part of the marriage. Keep in mind that abuse is not just physical; it is emotional and verbal.

• *Trust is gone.* There have been repeated infidelities or abuses, or your addicted spouse refuses to go into or stay in a recovery program. You know you cannot trust your spouse to do the right thing—that promises mean nothing. No marriage can be built on lies.

• *Your spouse is indifferent.* "This is your problem, not mine. I don't have a problem." Apathy is a sure killer of any hope for a healthy marriage.

• *Reality has asserted itself.* All your denials, wishes, hopes, and magic thinking have been swept away. You see clearly that what you have is not a marriage, but mere cohabitation.

• *Your spouse has no interest in having a real marriage.* Your spouse acknowledges there are problems, but wants to stay married for reasons unrelated to the relationship like money considerations or for the children's sake.

• *All efforts to save your marriage have been unilateral.* Your spouse has made little or no effort, and may even laugh at or deride your efforts. You cannot simply work harder at it all by yourself. At some point, no amount of pleading, enabling, even praying is going to help.

You Must Make a Decision

Some of us are ready to make decisions quickly, for others it may take some time. But God will see to it that you become so uncomfortable with inaction, you will not be able to continue. Perhaps you feel that things will straighten themselves out if you just give them time. How much time? The question is: How long can you go on pretending and suffering? Should you have to?

One reason for paralysis at decision time is we are afraid of making a mistake. You can always undo a mistake. If you file for divorce and your spouse wakes up suddenly and sincerely wants to work on things, if shock and awe are what it takes, so be it. But you know in your heart whether that has much chance of happening. You know your spouse better than anyone on earth. Now be honest. Is it over?

You cannot back off because the thought of divorce gives you hives. You cannot back off because you are in pain. Pain is what it takes to wake us up. You cannot back off because you will be the one blamed. Ask yourself, and be honest: Is it over?

For Reflection

1. Where are you with your decision to divorce? Are you ready to make that decision? Have you divorced already, but are not completely ready to move on?

_____

_____

_____

_____

_____

2. If you have made your decision or are divorced already, how did you hear from God? How has that decision been confirmed as time has gone on?

_____

_____

_____

_____

_____

3. What signs that your efforts were failing led you to decide divorce was the only alternative? Was there a crisis? Or was the realization gradual?

_____

_____

_____

_____

_____

4. Take some time to write your own thoughts.

_____

_____

_____

_____

_____

_____

_____

_____

_____

_____

_____

_____

_____

part two

THE

JOURNEY

THROUGH

DIVORCE

When you pass through the waters, I will be with you;
and through the rivers, they shall not overwhelm you…

Because you are precious in my sight,
and honored, and I love you…
—Isaiah 43:2, 4

chapter five

LEANING ON LOVE

Thus says the LORD who made you,
who formed you in the womb
and will help you:
Do not fear…
—Isaiah 44:2

Your decision has been made. You are going to be divorced or you're already divorced. This part is a relief; uncertainty and indecision are stressful. Now that the decision is made, you have to go through with it, and it will not be quick or easy. It is not easy to be awake, face reality, and do the right thing. But the alternative is a kind of death. You have been in the darkness long enough. Coming into the light of truth is painful. You may have doubts that you even like the light, but it will be well worth it.

First, do not be afraid. Remember you are not alone. You sought God to help make your decision. You are doing what you believe to be the right thing. God is close to the broken-hearted, Isaiah 61:1 assures us. Your relationship with God is about to rise to a new level. Your decision to divorce, while painful, is a courageous one. We who stay in bad marriages for a long time are really good people, spiritual people who care about God and others. We want to do the most loving thing. Divorce may seem like the most unloving thing we could possibly do. In actuality, it may be the most loving thing, both for ourselves and for our spouse. None of us grows in angry, false, codependent, indifferent relationships.

Your decision to divorce is going to cause negative reactions. Your spouse, in spite of everything, may act astonished that you would make such a choice. Your in-laws may become hostile. Some of your friends won't support you. Later chapters will guide you in telling others of your decision, briefly and clearly, then walking away and avoiding empty talk or explanations.

You will be heartened by those who do rally around you. When I was going through my divorce, God gathered around me a wonderful group of people, who were like a warm quilt on a cold night. Some were old friends I had lost touch with; some were brand-new friends. They propped me up, prayed for me, held my hand, and gave me hugs, pep talks, and good advice.

You will look back on this as a time of tremendous spiritual growth, a complete turning point in your life. As you go through it, it won't be fun. But think about it: What have you been going through for the last years or decades? Deep in your heart, you knew this could not go on. Wasn't part of you dying little by little? It isn't easy. We get comfortable with the little hells we make for ourselves. But God insists that we be free, that we come into the light, that we grow up.

Helplessness

Of all the emotions you may be experiencing, helplessness or feeling out of control may be the most dominant. This is perfectly normal, and there's good news about that feeling. Helplessness is one of the greatest spiritual resources we can have. Author Catherine Marshall writes that these times should be welcomed as a gift from God:

> ...our human helplessness is bedrock fact. God is a realist and insists that we be realists too. So long as we are deluding ourselves that human resources can supply our heart's desires, we are believing a lie. And it is impossible for prayers to be answered out of a foundation of self-deception and untruth.[1]

As long as we are relying on ourselves, feeling in control, running our own show, we don't feel helpless, but we also cannot draw close to God or understand God's love and power. Our self-reliance, our independence from God, blocks any real spiritual growth. It may have been the chief reason our marriages failed.

Jesus made a startling statement about himself, recorded in the Gospel of John: "...the Son can do nothing on his own, but only what he sees the Father doing..." (5:19). Jesus is God. If Jesus speaks this way, why do we believe we will be fine on our own without God?

Going through divorce is a great training ground in relying on God. We experience a good, holy helplessness that will show us the importance of leaning on God. If you are feeling helpless, if life seems to be spinning out of control, turn it all over to God, and trust that you will be cared for and guided in your decisions over these next months—and for the rest of your life.

The Dark Forest

When I started down the long road to divorce, I felt as though I was descending into a dark forest, going down a faint path I could barely see. It was scary, but somehow I felt safer and calmer than I had in a long time. There was something about *knowing* this was right, that this was the decision I had to make, calmed me. There was no more wondering, confusion, false hopes. The marriage was over. Walking in the woods isn't so bad if God keeps us company.

Let's go on and see what is ahead.

For Reflection

1. How did you feel when the decision to divorce was made? Relieved? Grieved? Calm? Afraid? All of the above?

_____

_____

_____

_____

2. Are you feeling helpless, or did you feel helpless when you first decided to get divorced? Are you willing to let God guide you through this?

_____

_____

_____

_____

_____

3. What metaphor would you use to describe your feelings now or when you first made the decision to divorce?

_____

_____

_____

_____

_____

4. Take some time to write your own thoughts.

_____

_____

_____

_____

_____

_____

_____

_____

_____

_____

_____

_____

_____

chapter six

TAKING CARE OF YOURSELF

We are not the sum of our weaknesses and failures,
we are the sum of the Father's love.
—Pope John Paul II. World Youth Day,
Toronto, Canada, 2002[1]

Once you have made the divorce decision, there are some practical things that need to be done. Here's what I did first: I took off my wedding ring and put it and all my jewelry in my own safety deposit box. I moved out of our marital bedroom into a spare bedroom, and tried to make it a cheerful, private retreat. I withdrew money from a joint account and retained a lawyer. I opened my own checking and savings accounts. I gathered financial records, made copies of everything, and kept them at a friend's office.

My biggest challenge was keeping myself well, physically and mentally. I was suffering from clinical depression, and that had to be treated, just like any other medical condition.

I needed to stay awake and alert, to get up every morning and put one foot in front of the other. My job as a newspaper reporter and my college courses were helpful. My coworkers, professors, and fellow students knew about my situation and supported me. The work and study kept me distracted and busy most of the day. Evenings were difficult, though. I was very reluctant to go home at the end of the day, but again,

I stayed busy doing coursework or reading. I found music very sooth-ing. And I had a large Dalmatian who seemed to know what was hap-pening and insisted on hug-and-play therapy.

Taking care of yourself during this tough time is imperative. More than likely, you will be living with your spouse in the same house dur-ing legal negotiations. It takes patience and courtesy to live with some-one you are about to divorce. This is "in-house separation." You will have to agree upon separate times to use the kitchen and other common areas, and your bedrooms should be absolutely off-limits to one another. Each of you needs a private place where you know you will not be dis-turbed.

Have any discussions in a neutral place and by appointment. If you cannot have calm talks at home, conduct negotiations in a public place or in one of your lawyers' offices. If you feel there is any threat of phys-ical abuse, you must get a restraining order and get your spouse ordered out of the house. Usually, though, the biggest challenge is to be patient while the slow legal process goes on. The trick is to keep praying, stay busy with something you enjoy doing, and spend time with friends and family who will support you and make you laugh.

Take Care of Your Body

Nothing beats the temptation to melancholy like getting regular exer-cise. Take walks, join an exercise class, or go to a gym, but get yourself moving. Exercise will also help your appetite and your sleep.

Put yourself on a regimen of healthy, low-fat foods, including a lot of fruits and vegetables and enough protein. Call this your "divorce diet" and think of it as food to give you strength to get through this time. Eating comfort food high in fat and sugar may feel good for a while, but will only make you sluggish and irritable later.

Get enough sleep. Set up a calming bedtime routine for yourself. Hot milk, a bowl of oatmeal, any carbohydrate-loaded food will help you sleep. Get into bed and read for a while. Your before-bed reading should be absorbing, but not too exciting. Poetry, travel books, or long, rambling novels are wonderful. Buy yourself a sound machine that plays soothing nature sounds.

You are going to need some physical touch at this time. The loss of whatever physical intimacy you were used to in marriage can cause depression. We are physical beings, so we need physical touch. Ask for hugs from friends. Ask for a back rub from a friend or one of your children. Get a professional massage. Sit in a hot tub and let the jets pummel you. You'll be surprised how a little physical touch will cheer you up.

Take Care of Your Mind

Your first line of defense for your mental health is going to be counseling. You need to talk out your feelings and begin the work of healing from the marriage and what led up to the marriage. Now is the time to begin.

One caution: Do not, under any circumstances, use your children (of any age, but especially young children) as your counselors. This is totally inappropriate and unfair to them. Neither you nor your spouse should be confiding in your children. They have their own issues with your divorce; do not put any added burdens on them. Whether you intend it or not, they will feel they need to take sides. Each of you needs to talk your problems and issues out with an objective adult, a trained professional, either a psychologist, psychiatrist, counselor, or clergy member.

I find journaling to be my best source of mental wellness. I write and write when I am angry, confused, depressed. By the time I have written a few pages, I have worked my way through the problem. Lots of times, I find God speaking to me through my pen, giving advice, making observations, helping me see things I couldn't see before.

Dealing with your emotions is the biggest challenge of going through a divorce. The best way to deal with loneliness, anger, grief, fear, guilt, and all the rest, is to face them boldly. That may be hard if you are used to denying your feelings. But you need to face them, to say, "I feel very angry / lonely / frightened right now." You need to examine your feelings and to talk with God about them. Emotions lose their control over you when you pull them into the light, look at them closely, accept them as part of your landscape at this time. Avoidance and denial only give emotions more strength to hurt you deep inside. If you force them into the light and scrutinize them, they lose much of their power.

Take Care of Your Spirit

The most practical thing I know to do for my spirit is to take a Sabbath every week. In this busy culture of ours, do any of us have time to take a whole day off just to do…nothing? Of course not. That's why we must do it.

Start taking one day a week as a Sabbath. Do no work, studying, poring over legal documents. Give up your worries for the day, too. Spend the day however you like. I was in college when I began this practice, so it was a delight to spend my Sabbaths napping and reading books that were not required for my classes. I read children's books, mysteries, poetry. I chatted on the phone. I played with the dog. I just enjoyed myself. Yes, and I prayed also, but it was easy and relaxed prayer, very natural and pleasant.

I have kept to my Sabbath practice every week since 2002. Sabbath-keeping has helped me draw closer to God than any other practice I know. Think of it: What is more precious to us than our time? When we give our Sabbath time to God, who immediately gives it back to us in the form of rest and play, we are not only obeying the Sabbath commandment, we are also refreshing ourselves and equipping ourselves for the rigors of the week ahead.

In this stressful time of your life, you need to take as good care of yourself as possible, to be as kind to yourself as you would a dear friend who is under the weather and in need of pampering.

More than anything, you need to take care of that tired, perhaps guilt-ridden and defeated person that is you right now. And you need to remind yourself of Pope John Paul II's wisdom: You are not the sum of your weaknesses, but the sum of your Father's love.

For Reflection

1. What survival strategies in this chapter do you find most helpful in your situation, or would have been helpful in the first months after your divorce decision?

_____

_____

_____

_____

_____

2. How do you handle your need for touch and intimacy now that you are single (or about to be single)?

_____

_____

_____

_____

_____

3. How do you feel about taking a Sabbath every week? Do you feel this is impossible? Are you willing to give it a try?

_____

_____

_____

_____

_____

4. Take some time to write your own thoughts.

_____

_____

_____

_____

_____

_____
_____
_____
_____
_____
_____
_____
_____
_____
_____
_____
_____
_____
_____
_____
_____
_____
_____
_____
_____
_____
_____
_____
_____
_____
_____
_____
_____
_____
_____
_____

chapter seven

TELLING OTHERS

Let your word be "Yes, Yes" or "No, No"; anything
more than this comes from the evil one.
—Matthew 5:37

For lack of wood the fire goes out, and where
there is no whisperer, quarreling ceases.
—Proverbs 26:20

It's time to talk about…talking. How do you tell others that you are getting a divorce? Whom should you tell? How much should you tell?

Who Has the Right to Know?
There are certain people in your circle of family and friends who have
the most right to know what is going on, namely your children and your
parents. There are probably others in your circle—siblings, best friends,
even close coworkers—whom you will want to tell. Some of these people may be privy to your situation. But you may have been reluctant to
tell the others. In fact, you may be dreading these conversations, but you
will feel better afterward. And you will have their support and prayers
once you tell them.

Even though you may consider your in-laws family, it is best that
your spouse handles disclosing the divorce to his or her side of the family. As much as the temptation remains to tell your side of the story to

your in-laws, it is best to let your spouse handle the details (just as you would not want your spouse speaking to members of your family before you had a chance to speak to them).

There are others in your circle of acquaintances—not-so-close friends and family, neighbors, and coworkers, who will eventually need to know you are going to be divorced. Later in this chapter, we will consider the simple statement of fact that you will craft to inform these people. Let's concentrate on informing the people closest to you. This is one of the more difficult tasks of going through a divorce.

Telling Your Children

Both you and your spouse should sit down with your children and tell them together what is going on. First, this is your marriage that is failing. Perhaps the last act you will make as a married couple (aside from appearing in court together) will be to sit down with your children and explain that the marriage is ending.

There will be no accusing one another, assigning blame, even admitting fault in this conversation. You are conveying information, simply and carefully. Your children will be devastated enough (no matter what their age) without your acting like children yourselves, trying to draw sides, or giving them too much information. They don't need to hear about all your issues with one another. They need to know that you still love them and will be there for them, even if you aren't together as a couple any more.

This is why it is essential that you both be present when you break the news to your children. We are faulty humans and, during a divorce, want so much to justify ourselves and assign blame to the other. We cannot do this in front of our children. Being there together during the conversation will assure each of you that the other did not say something false or accusatory. If we need to rant, rage, and blame, we should do it in our counselor's office, or with a close friend. But we need to get beyond ranting, raging, and blaming.

You will, naturally, be concerned about your children's reactions, which will range from anger to confusion to depression. The best way to deal with your children's grief is to handle your own in an adult way. If they see that you are all right, they will be, too, eventually. If they see you acting like a child, they will do that, too. Remember how airlines tell parents to handle an emergency: Put on your own oxygen mask first, then help your child with his or hers.

This of course is an oversimplification of a very complicated issue. How one addresses a very young child or preschooler, a tween or a teenager, or even an adult child or a grown-up with children of their own with this news varies tremendously and may require further reading and research. Hit the library and try to a find a resource that addresses how to guide your children through the divorce process—which requires an entire book in and of itself.

Telling Parents and Siblings

As I mentioned earlier, each of you is in charge of informing your own families about your pending divorce, and the sooner the better. Again, be careful about what you say; the simple statement you will create later will help. If you assign all the blame for the divorce on your spouse, you may get lots of sympathy, but it's eventually going to get back to your children. I can guarantee that if your children hear nasty gossip from your side of the family, they will be less likely to want to be part of them. They will become protective of the other parent. So be careful, and consider the future—after this is over, after your emotions calm down; you do not want to be ashamed of your actions later.

Toxic People

We all love a juicy bit of gossip! A couple in the family or workplace or neighborhood or church getting a divorce, especially after a long marriage, is the juiciest tidbit there is. Accept the fact that some people will get interested in your situation all of a sudden. Some may never have been close to you before. They will want to know details, who did what to whom, who is to blame. They will be very sympathetic. And you may be very tempted to talk, and talk, and talk.

But understand this: This kind of talk is mere gossip. It is not the healthy, healing process you need to go through when a marriage ends. It will not help you, and it may actually damage you and interfere with your healing.

You know who you can trust with your hurts and confidences: your counselor and closest family and friends. These people are not interested in gossip, only in helping you get through this. Keep your thoughts to yourself with everyone else. Resist the urge to get drawn in, to justify yourself, to make yourself feel better. Conversations with toxic, gossipy people never help, never make you feel better. You only come away feeling more hurt and angry.

If someone asks you a personal question "What happened?" "Is he cheating on you?" "Is she drinking again?" "Did you try _____?" Do what columnist Ann Landers always advised. Stare at them for a moment and ask, "Why do you want to know?" or "Why would you ask that?" If they don't take the hint, say, "I don't want to talk about it."

The Simple Statement of Fact
My psychologist helped me come up with a simple statement that I used to tell people that I was about to divorce after three decades of marriage. It worked like a charm. It shut up gossips, kept me from talking too much, and helped me steer the conversation into safer waters. Here is how you construct your own:

The statement is "I cannot stay in a/an _____ marriage." Since you have already read nearly half of this book, you should be able to think of a suitable adjective to fill in the blank. Here are some to choose from: *failed; fake; indifferent; stagnant; silent; uncommitted; unforgiving; unhealthy; unloving; unreal; unworkable.* You may only pick one or two, not all eleven.

This is simple to memorize, and keeps things unemotional. Your assignment, right now, is to consider what your statement of fact will be and who you need to tell that you are getting a divorce. Get through this step with your head high and your emotions in control, and you will feel a lot better.

Learn to Keep Silence

Once you tell those who have the right to know that you are divorcing, you must learn to say very little, except to those who are in your confidence. You can vent all you want to your counselor, to God, in your journal, to a few close friends, but learn to be quiet around everyone else.

Keeping silence, especially at this time, is a good spiritual discipline. It may be opposite what you want to do, especially if you are an extrovert like me. But silence is healing. There comes a time when talking it out does not work anymore. It only makes you feel worse.

Silence is a form of prayer. Silence allows you to hear God speaking to you, comforting you, guiding you. Again, I say, silence heals. When we stop compulsively talking, when we enter into God's silence, we can access those deep waters within us, what Jesus called "living waters" flowing from the center of our being. During all our marital problems, the years when we were trying so hard to keep things together, we may have lost sight of that deeper part of us. Silence will help restore us.

For Reflection

1. Decide on your simple statement and memorize it. Even if you have been divorced for a long time, this is still a good exercise.

_____

_____

_____

_____

_____

2. Make three concentric circles and label them: "Closest and Dearest;" "Close but Not Dearest;" and "Other Family/Friends." Write the names

of all your loved ones and acquaintances in the proper circles. How much information does each group need or have a right to know about your divorce?

_____

_____

_____

_____

_____

3. If you have children, how much information do you feel comfortable telling them about your divorce? When will you and your spouse sit down and talk with them? How will you assure them of your love for them? If you are already divorced, how did you handle this task?

_____

_____

_____

_____

_____

4. Take some time to write your own thoughts.

_____

_____

_____

_____

_____

_____

_____

_____

_____

chapter eight

GRIEVING WHEN IT'S OVER

All those years I fell for the great palace lie that grief should
be gotten over as quickly as possible and as privately.
But what I've discovered since is that the lifelong fear of
grief keeps us in a barren, isolated place and that only
grieving can heal grief…
—Anne Lamott, *Traveling Mercies: Some Thoughts on Faith*[1]

You may be surprised, as I was, at the power of your grief right now. But,
think about it. While you were in the pre-divorce stage, negotiating,
dividing, moving out or helping the spouse move out, you felt a lot of
things. Anger, frustration, impatience. There was not much time for
grief. When it's over, the grief sets in.

We who are divorced have lost so much: The person we gave our lives
to, the life we were used to, the future we expected. Take the time to
grieve. If you skip this step, you will never fully recover, never really heal
and be able to go on with life.

Balance your grief by accepting those moments, which will become
more frequent, when you feel calm, peaceful, even happy—when you
know you are free, and your life stretches out in front of you, full of
promise and opportunities.

Sometimes, after a trauma like a divorce, we think we should not be
happy, we don't deserve serenity and satisfaction. We may find ourselves

missing the emotions, the anger and angst because we lived that way for so long. But it's time to pull away from all that, from getting a rise from all the excitement and drama that may have been part of our lives for years.

Emotions after a divorce are extremely volatile, swinging from loneliness and grief one minute to anger the next to happiness that it's all over, at last. This is perfectly normal. You have just been through about the worst trauma there is. Be gentle and kind to yourself now, and you will eventually come to a calmer, steadier state of mind.

The Ritual of Transition

Is it all right to celebrate your divorce? Why not, if it's done quietly and for a good, constructive purpose?

There are several good reasons for having a get-together with a few close friends to mark your transition as a single person:

- to mark this major passage in your life,
- to strengthen your support system (and remind yourself that you have one),
- to reconnect, after being disconnected for too long.

So, go ahead, gather some good friends, and have a quiet get-together after your divorce is final. Ask each friend to write you an encouraging letter to reread in the months ahead. Write each of them a note thanking them for their support, and be specific about what actions helped you the most. Listen to some good music, pray together, have a meal. Do whatever you want to do, except gossip or get wildly drunk. Talk about the future, talk about what you might want to do now that you are free, enlist your friends' support. Just hang out and enjoy yourself, basking in the love of these people God has sent you.

Human beings have marked major passages in life for millennia. We have elaborate ceremonies, religious and secular, to mark birth, coming of age, graduation, marriage, anniversaries, and finally, death. Divorce is seldom acknowledged, much less observed with a ceremony. We all feel terrible that marriages fail. But this is a life passage, just like the death of a spouse. Divorced people need to be supported, loved, and helped to go forward to healing and wholeness.

A ritual of transition helps us move forward, safe in the knowledge that we are loved and appreciated, not only by our friends and family, but by God.

Healing Exercises

While healing from a failed marriage and going through the process of grief take time and patience, there are some things you can do to cooperate with the process.

One of the first things I did after my divorce was go through old photo albums and scrapbooks. You must do this with lots of time for privacy and a large box of tissues, but it is very healing. I took a retrospective tour of our entire marital relationship, depicted in photos, letters, ticket stubs. I wept over it all, pulled the albums apart, and divided everything into "his" and "hers." I put my ex-husband's family photos into a bag and had one of my sons deliver it to him. This was one of the more painful things I did after my divorce, but it was healing in unexpected ways. I rediscovered some of the missing "me" I had lost in the years of the marriage. It helped me close a door to the past and move on to the future.

Finding Your Dreams Again

During the long years of your marriage and then the months or years going through divorce proceedings, what happened to your dreams? If you are typical, your goals, dreams, and creative desires were left behind, put off because you had too many worries and too little encouragement.

In Mary Chapin Carpenter's song, "My Pirate Days," she admits burying all her dreams for another to find. Is that what happened to you? Do you have buried dreams that you have long neglected?

I certainly did. I wanted badly to be a freelance writer, but that was never going to happen in the last years of my marriage. There was too much static, too many hurts, worries, and fears to concentrate on being creative. Since my divorce, I have recovered my creativity. I'm a full-time writer. I sing in a community chorale. I've even started sewing again, something I haven't done for decades.

Dreams are wonderful things. You can bury them for years and years. Then you can find where you buried them, apply some water (tears?), and you will find that, instead of rotting as you would expect, they are perfectly good. Dreams are more like seeds. Here in the desert where I live, there are certain seeds that lay dormant in the ground for years and years, waiting for a hard rainstorm on just the right day to sprout and come into the open. The desert in bloom is glorious. Your heart in bloom will also be splendid.

Your dreams are waiting for you. What did you long to do before your divorce? Did you, too, want to write or create, sing or play a musical instrument? Or did you like gardening, crafting, decorating, but never had the time or the emotional energy?

God wants your dreams to come true. God will cheer you on when you explore your creative side and do the risky things that aren't on your daily to do list. God is the creator, and you are made in that image. Part of you will die if you never create, especially if you don't create because you are too busy or because your troubles squeeze the creativity out.

It's time to water those dreams of yours.

In a journal entry I wrote shortly after my divorce, I was impatient. I wanted the grief to be over, wanted to feel better now, wanted to know what was going to happen to me. "I want some assurance of what the future is going to be," I wrote. "Everything seems so risky now. I'm looking for some kind of security…"

Life can seem risky during times like this. But God is here in our present, and goes ahead of us to our future, clearing the way for us. We are safe.

For I am convinced that neither death, nor life, nor angels, nor rulers, nor things present, nor things to come, nor powers, nor height, nor depth, nor anything else in all creation, will be able to separate us from the love of God in Christ Jesus our Lord. (Romans 8:38–39)

For Reflection

1. Are you (or were you) surprised at the depth of your grief after divorce?

_____

_____

_____

_____

_____

_____

2. Does a "ritual of transition" sound like a good idea to you? If so, who would you invite and what would you like to do?

_____

_____

_____

_____

_____

_____

3. Do you feel you buried a lot of dreams during your marriage? What were they?

_____

_____

_____

_____

_____

4. Take some time to write your own thoughts.

_____
_____
_____
_____
_____
_____
_____
_____
_____
_____
_____
_____
_____
_____
_____
_____
_____
_____
_____
_____
_____
_____
_____
_____
_____
_____
_____
_____
_____
_____
_____
_____

part three

CREATING

A

LIFE

OF

YOUR

OWN

For surely I know the plans I have for you, says the LORD,
plans for your welfare and not for harm,
to give you a future with hope.
—Jeremiah 29:11

chapter nine

LEARNING TO LIVE LOVED

Whatever has happened, we are still called to holiness,
we are still called to love those around us. We are thus
called to give witness to the one love that never fails or
deserts us: the love God has for us.
—Seán Wales, *Catholics and Divorce:*
Finding Help and Healing Within the Church[1]

As human beings and children of God, our whole lives are spent return-
ing to God and learning to live as though we are loved by God, because
we are. This is tough for most of us. For us divorced folk, it may seem
impossible to remember or believe we are loved. Our hearts are heavy,
our love rejected, our emotions shattered.

But we are loved by God. We may not be able to feel it yet, but that
does not change reality. God has always loved us, loves us now, will love
us forever. No matter what we do, what choices we make, God loves us,
because God is love and, therefore, cannot stop loving us.

The title for this chapter comes from William Paul Young's best-
selling book, *The Shack*. In this fictional account of a grieving father's
weekend with God at a cabin in the woods, all three members of the
Trinity are present, sharing meals with Young's alter-ego, Mack, and con-
versing about issues that affect all of us. Mack is grieving the loss of his
four-year-old daughter who was murdered. He is understandably angry,

distrustful, judgmental, confused, and weary. He wants to be healed, but has no idea how to go about it.

In one of the more touching conversations between Mack and God (in the guise of a large African American woman), a little bird flies in the window and sits on God's finger. God tells Mack that birds were created to fly, that being grounded is a limitation of a bird's natural, God-given ability to soar. She tells Mack:

> You, on the other hand, were created to be loved. So for you to live as if you were unloved is a limitation. . . . Living unloved is like clipping a bird's wings and removing its ability to fly. Not something I want for you. . . . Mack, pain has a way of clipping our wings and keeping us from being able to fly. . . And if left unresolved for very long, you can almost forget that you were ever created to fly in the first place.[2]

Those words leapt off the page at me: I was created to be loved! The stress and strain of an unloving marriage and its final, painful end had caused mental depression and physical problems. But the worst thing was the spiritual illness my divorce caused. The failure of marital love obstructed my ability to see God's love. Like Mack in the book, my "wings" had been clipped. I not only forgot how to fly; I forgot I was meant to fly.

More than likely, you feel the same way; you feel your wings have been clipped and you have forgotten how to be happy and free—how to fly. How do we recover? How do we understand that, in spite of all we've been through, we are loved?

The answer is not what we think it would be. In our culture today, we solve our problems by setting goals and working toward solutions by our own efforts. That will not work in our situation. "Learning to live loved" is not going to happen by our doing; it will only happen when we give up doing and learn to be. Only God can heal us. We cannot heal ourselves by willpower, by trying to create feelings of love, by talking ourselves into believing it.

The story of the woman at the well in the Gospel of John is helpful here. This woman must be the most famous divorcee of the Bible: She had been married five times and, when Jesus met her, she had apparently given up on the marriage thing and was simply living with her man. This was a woman in need of healing. Jesus saw that. He also saw that she was open to what God wanted to tell her.

And what did Jesus tell this woman? "You have to stop being naughty and obey the rules"? No. "You have to have some goals in life, get some self-discipline"? No.

Jesus said, in effect, "I have something you need: Living water. Water that will make you stop thirsting for the wrong type of love. Water that will satisfy you forever. Water that will gush up within you, washing your sins away, making you new, making you free."

I understand that woman's excitement. I understand why she ran back to the village and told everyone to come and see this man that was sitting by the village well. She may not have understood what Jesus was talking about at first, but in her heart, she knew he had what she needed, what we all need. The living water Jesus speaks of is himself. He is the only one who can satisfy our longing to be loved, who can heal our wounded hearts, who can make us free. Free enough to fly again, to be who we were meant to be. To know we are loved, and to live loved.

Our part in our own healing is less active than we are comfortable with in this culture. Perhaps the only active part we can take is to be intentional about meeting God at the well. We need to show up at our daily devotional time, to slow down and make time for God and ourselves.

Slowing down is tough for us in these days. It's not natural for us. We are busy, and we like to stay busy. After the trauma we've been through, staying busy may seem like a good idea. We don't want to face our loneliness, our sadness, our anger. We don't want to tone down all the noise in our lives because noise is an anesthetic, and silence is uncomfortable.

But the work of healing has to take place in the silent place, away from the crowds and noise and busyness. There is deep work to do, work in the recesses of our hearts where we cannot reach. There are dams and blockages in there that prevent the living water from flowing through us. So, we have to learn to sit for some time every day. We must learn to still ourselves, to spend quiet time with God every day. Many times, we will feel nothing is happening, no healing is going on in here, it's all a waste of time. But give God the time, and the healing will happen. You will notice little things at first. You will begin to feel happier, maybe for a few minutes at first, then for longer periods, then almost all the time. You'll feel the blockages inside clearing and the living water flowing through you, cleansing you, making you feel light and free. You will start to feel loved, again just a little at first, then most of the time.

You cannot manage your own healing. This is not your area of expertise. This is God's specialty. All you can do is show up, be open and accepting, follow the paths where God leads you. You may read Scripture and journal as part of your healing. You may go to counseling. You may weep a lot. Or you may just sit, feeling nothing, but letting God work in your deepest heart.

Remember that your healing and ultimate perfection is the work of God, especially the work of the Holy Spirit. We did not create ourselves, and we cannot repair or remake ourselves after divorce. All we can do is position ourselves to receive God's healing, transformative love. We can say no to the urge to run away from our pain and bring that pain to God. And God, being the great healer, will do what God does best.

For Reflection

1. *I not only forgot how to fly; I forgot I was meant to fly.* Has your divorce made you feel this way? Explain.

_____

_____

2. Read the story of the woman at the well in the fourth chapter of John's Gospel. Imagine yourself in her position. What would you say to Jesus when he talked about giving you living water? What questions would you have? How would you respond to his invitation?

_____

_____

_____

_____

_____

3. Do you think you can learn to live loved? Are you willing to give God the time every day in order to be healed and loved?

_____

_____

_____

_____

_____

4. Take some time to write your own thoughts.

_____

_____

_____

_____

_____

_____

_____

_____

chapter ten

MAKING FIRST DECISIONS

A life should be as carefully planned as a work of art... What
image of yourself have you been secretly entertaining? Bring
the image out of the closet, entertain it consciously...
—Kenneth Atchity, *A Writer's Time: A Guide to the Creative
Process from Vision through Revision*[1]

A few months before my divorce was final, I was sitting with the Lord
during my prayer time and feeling little except numbness. Actually, the
numbness was a relief. I usually felt just awful: grief-stricken, crazy, anxious, nervous. Numbness was an improvement over my usual state.

Then I heard God's voice in my heart, speaking so clearly, there could
be no mistake. "Have you decided to live?" Strange question, I thought.
That's one of the ways I know God is speaking to me: He says things I
would never, in a million years, say to myself.

God's question was a good one. I had not been "living" in the fullest
sense for at least two years while all the divorce drama was going on. I
had been emoting, trembling in fear, numb with pain, disbelieving,
angry...but I wasn't living.

Isn't it amazing how God knows just what to say to cut through all the
garbage we pile on ourselves?

"Have you decided to live?"

The question brought me back to myself and woke me up.

I began to think about it. What does it mean to go on living after life as we know it ends? Is it enough to drift through our days, waiting for the next blow, fearing what is going to happen to us, vacillating between emotional chaos and numbness?

God's question helped me see I needed to come back to life. I could make plans and have goals. I needed to make the best choices I could for my future. I would not be part of a couple, deferring to another. That felt odd after marriage, but it also felt kind of exciting. That excitement made me feel a little guilty, but there it was, welling up inside me. I could begin to construct a new life, and I felt a small glimmer of hope that it could be a good one.

As I sat there thinking all this, I made my first tentative decision as a soon-to-be-single person: I wanted to keep the house we had been living in. Since we were just beginning negotiations for our legal settlement, this was an important decision. But at that moment, all I knew was that I just wanted to stay there, to fix it up, to make it mine.

Years later, I could have questioned that decision. Repairs had cost a lot of money. I was trying to sell it just as the housing market in my area crashed. In the end, a neighbor bought it for much less than I paid for my new home in Arizona. Should I have made a different decision? I don't think so. I needed to exercise my ability to choose when God asked, "Have you decided to live?" I needed to think about my future, my preferences. That was what I wanted then. I did not need to know what the future was going to be. God and I dealt with those realities when the time came. In retrospect, it was the right decision.

Our decisions right now, at the end of one life and the beginning of another, may not turn out perfectly. We worry about that, especially when marriage ends and we are faced with constructing new lives all on our own. But any decision that expresses what is in our hearts and who we are right now, is the right decision. We can always make another decision later. We have that freedom now.

So, what about you? Have you decided to live again?

Fear of Failure

It is normal to feel hesitant and uncertain at this time of life. For some of us, it may have been years since we asserted ourselves. During our marriages, we may have tiptoed around, afraid to make a decisive move because it would trigger a confrontation. Certainly, our self-esteem has taken a beating when the biggest decision we ever made—to marry—turned out so badly. We may feel reluctant to even pick out a paint color for the living room right now, feeling stupid and self-conscious. But feelings of failure are just that—feelings. They are not real. We are not stupid for choosing the person we chose. We were doing the best we could at the time. God doesn't hold our decision against us. Why do we punish ourselves so?

Our fear of making decisions and of living again is rooted in a fear of failure. Coupled with that is our culture's obsession with perfection. We have this perception that there is a right way and a wrong way to do everything. We don't want to do the wrong thing again, so we back away from choosing anything. By doing that, we are backing away from life.

It's time to live again. It's time to be who we are, to determine our own path in life. Everything from how we decorate our living quarters to where we live and work are ours to choose. It may seem overwhelming, but choices are made simply, one at a time. We don't have to make all our decisions right now. We do have to decide to take up life again and live it.

It's OK to make mistakes, even to do things badly. What we need to do right now is get moving, get living. Your new life is in the first draft stage. That's all right. You can always revise later.

The One Decision You Should Make Right Now

I feel compelled to make one point about post-divorce decisions. We will cover this more completely later in "Building a Good Foundation," but there is one post-divorce move you should not even consider right now. That is the decision to look for another mate, to "hook up," even to date. It seems silly to have to mention that, but that is the first thing a lot of divorced (both men and women) do. My interviews for this book have made it obvious that even committed Christians jump right back into the dating scene right after divorce, often with disastrous results. It's just too soon.

We need an appropriate period of reflection and healing after divorce. This is not the time to be looking for someone new. We are not up to that, and we are certainly not up to the additional beating our spirits will take if this relationship fails. We need to protect ourselves better than that.

The reality about relationships is this: We will only attract to ourselves (and be attracted to) someone who is as healed as we are. How healed do you think you are right now? What sort of person do you suppose would be attracted to you?

When I was first divorced, I knew I would have been attracted to anyone who was remotely nice to me, anyone who said the right things to make me feel better about myself. I also knew that there are men out there who have a kind of radar, who can pick up the signs of a woman in distress, like a shark picking up the signals from a dying fish. Since I did not feel like being eaten by a shark, I stayed away from men, from singles groups, from even thinking about dating for two years after my divorce. After that, my head was a lot clearer, I wasn't so needy, I wasn't giving out those dangerous vibes to the single sharks. I also discovered that I really like being single, that any man I would consider spending time with would have to be very special, indeed.

Consider how wounded you feel right now, how hard life can be some days, maybe most days. You need time. Free time, away from the pressures and complications of an opposite-sex, romantic relationship. Make a decision that you will give yourself plenty of time, that you will post an invisible "don't bother" sign on you as you heal.

That will be the best post-divorce decision you can make. I guarantee you will never regret that one.

For Reflection

1. Does the question "Have you decided to live?" apply to you today?

_____

_____

_____

_____

_____

2. Since your divorce, have you felt hesitant and uncertain about your decisions? What simple and immediate decisions do you need to make today?

_____

_____

_____

_____

_____

3. Do you have a fear of failure and/or a feeling that you need to make perfect decisions? Can you let go of those feelings, make some choices, and be content to let them be imperfect?

_____

_____

_____

_____

_____

4. Are you willing to make a decision not to date for a while after your divorce is final? What might be the advantages of making this decision?

_____

_____

_____

_____

_____

5. Take some time to write your own thoughts.

_____
_____
_____
_____
_____
_____
_____
_____
_____
_____
_____
_____
_____
_____
_____
_____
_____
_____
_____
_____
_____
_____
_____
_____
_____
_____
_____
_____

chapter eleven

FORGIVING...EVERYONE

Before we forgive, we are handicapped, not able to do
what we could if we were free. We spend a lot of time
and energy better used elsewhere.
—Susan K. Rowland, *Make Room for God:*
Clearing Out the Clutter[1]

Two years after my divorce, I wrote an interesting entry in my journal. I had just attended a friend's funeral. I had also been trying unsuccessfully to sell my house for eighteen months. My journal records that I had a major temper tantrum that day and smashed up my telephone handset, although I don't recall the reason (a telephone solicitor?). I do recall smashing the phone—and I remember that it felt good, but it also felt scary. I'm not usually the destructive type. Bear in mind, this was two years after the divorce.

Realizing I was not exactly in control of myself, I went outside to try to calm down.

And God was out there to meet me.

How do I know that? You can always tell. God's presence was pressing on me, all around me. And I heard that "small, still voice" the Bible mentions: "We need to talk, honey."

A string of excuses and justifications for my tantrum rose in my mind, but God is never as interested in what precipitates an emotional reaction as what is underneath it all. What huge beach ball of anger had I been holding underwater that had just popped to the surface?

A few minutes of contemplation were all that was needed to figure this out: I still hadn't forgiven my ex-husband for everything that had happened to us, to me. My anger was always bubbling just below the surface. It was his fault that I was alone, dealing with a house that wouldn't sell. It was his fault that the house wouldn't sell. Heck, it was his fault that we bought the blasted house in the first place. My reasoning wasn't exactly honest. But it showed my state of mind at the time. The refusal to forgive is based on a lot of factors, some true, some half-true, some patently false.

Usually, when we refuse to forgive, we are getting some sort of benefit from not forgiving. We get to blame the other person instead of facing our own feelings of failure. We get to stay angry and agitated and excited instead of facing our grief or boredom. Forgiveness is really the last good-bye to the marriage, to that person who shared our lives. If we don't forgive, we can hold on to something of the past, even if it's entirely negative and evil. Like my smashing up the telephone, non-forgiveness can feel good, but it's an unhealthy way to live.

If we are to go on to a new and healthier life, to a life of freedom in God, we have to deal with our forgiveness issues. We have been hurt, we have been rejected, of course. Why else would we need to forgive? But we continue to hurt ourselves and block God's healing when we refuse to let go of the ones who have hurt us.

Closure

Part of the reason I found it hard to forgive my ex-husband was that I felt there was no real closure after my divorce. My inability to forgive was all tied up with not feeling any emotional finality. My ex and I still had to communicate with regard to the children. I still lived in the house we had shared, and I couldn't sell it when I wanted, so I felt stuck there. I still hurt. I still found myself going over and over what had happened, wondering and wishing things had been different. I thought I would be able to forgive when I felt it was all over, and it never felt like it was over.

What I did not realize is that forgiveness was the closure I needed.

So, that very evening after I smashed my phone, I let it all go. I finally forgave. And, amazingly, I found what I was longing for. From that day forward, I had the peace I needed. I could talk with my ex-husband. I could stay calm until I sold the house. Later, I could even accept that he had married again. Today, I still hurt at times; I still find myself wondering, imagining how it could have been different. But I've never been in that awful, scary place I was before I forgave. And I've never smashed up another phone.

Forgiveness and Pardon

There is a difference between forgiveness and pardon, although you won't find it in the dictionary. I learned this distinction from a book called *The One-Minute Philosopher*, by Dr. Montague Brown. I found this book just as I was going through my divorce, and it helped me tremendously with my confusion on this issue.

Here is the difference: Forgiveness is an internal thing. It takes place in the heart of the forgiver. It is a refusal to hold something against someone else in the heart. Forgiveness stops seeing a person as "the person who did _____ to me." Instead, it looks on that person as another frail human being, beset with all the same problems and needs that I have.

Pardon, on the other hand, is external, and may not involve forgiveness at all. In fact, people who do too much pardoning in their relationships often end up victimized and resentful. We have already discussed the normal consequence of long-term problems in a marriage, especially where there is abuse, addiction, adultery, indifference. The ultimate penalty of these actions is divorce, the refusal of the other spouse to be victimized any longer. Many of us "pardoned" our spouses for years and years, ignoring and denying the realities, probably enabling our spouse to become more and more irresponsible. At some point, we had to stop pardoning and allow the (natural) consequence of divorce to happen.

But we can still forgive. In fact, we must forgive.

The True Test of Forgiveness

Forgiving your ex-spouse is going to be a struggle, a very private battle you will fight in your own heart and mind. It will take time, although the moment you truly forgive may almost seem anti-climactic. You may wonder what took so long, why you held on so ferociously, why you didn't see the light sooner. Forgiveness is part of the whole healing process of divorce, of life. It takes time. God can't wave a magic wand over us and cure us instantaneously.

After we forgive, life becomes so much easier. The relief and peace that come after we have forgiven our ex are enough of a reward to want to continue forgiving everyone in our lives who has ever hurt us.

We cannot believe that forgiveness could ever feel that good before we do it. That is one of the proofs that we have forgiven. We experience forgiveness as a good and healing thing. Before we forgive, we imagine we will be defeating ourselves, that we will become less of a person if we let go. Afterward, we are in a totally different reality—God's reality. We finally understand.

My brother, Thom, a very wise person, says that the proof of forgiveness is this: We can pray for the one we forgive the same way we pray for ourselves. What kinds of things do we pray for ourselves? I pray for God to be close to me at all times, for peace in my heart, for good friends, for healing, for meaningful work, for safety. When I found myself able to pray those things for my ex-husband, I knew I had forgiven him.

It is painful to let someone go, especially when they have hurt us so deeply. We want our ex to make amends, to somehow give us back the years that were wasted, at least to acknowledge that we did our best. Often, they cannot. They are clueless, perhaps immature (aren't we all?). They have issues, too.

All that happens when we refuse to forgive is we become captives to ourselves. We hardly know where all the unrest and anger are coming from, but we know we are not at peace. Our anger, our holding on, becomes a steady stream of unhappiness that flows from some dark place within.

Jesus promised that living waters would flow from within us. Our refusal to forgive blocks the flow of God's love and grace within us. This is not something God wants to happen to us and, truthfully, it is not what we want for ourselves.

For Reflection

1. What progress are you making forgiving your ex-spouse? What signs are there in your life (such as sudden bursts of anger) that you may not have forgiven her or him entirely?

_____

_____

_____

_____

_____

2. What benefits or rationalizations do you see in yourself that make forgiveness difficult? Do you want closure? Do you feel forgiving would be proof of weakness? Do you see a connection between forgiveness and freedom?

_____

_____

_____

_____

_____

3. Take some time to write your own thoughts.

_____

_____

_____

_____

_____

chapter twelve

BUILDING A GOOD FOUNDATION

Divorce recovery is enhanced when we surround
ourselves with those who bring out the best in us
and help us on the journey toward inner peace.
—Barbara Leahy Shlemon[1]

Building a good foundation for post-divorce life means that God must
be the center of everything we do. A new, more mature, and more intentional relationship with God should be the goal. The only way to achieve
that is to be sure to give God some time every day and to keep faithful
to the practice of keeping Sabbath.

Another component of a healthy, happy life after divorce is our relationships, both with friends and with those we have left behind. Good,
supportive friends—companions on the journey—will help us heal and
grow spiritually. We will discuss post-divorce friendship below.

A mature, unemotional truce with our ex-spouses and their families is
also important. These people may still be a part of our lives. They will
certainly be taking up room in our heads for a long time! We do not
want to be dragged back into our painful pasts, into anger, regrets or
guilt every time we speak to or think about our ex or her or his family.
One way we can stop the negative feelings and time-wasting reveries is
to face our part in the marriage and divorce. That means facing our own

problems and perceptions, especially our childhood issues, that led to the problems in our marriage. We'll talk about that difficult task in this chapter, also.

Post-Divorce Friendships

Your friendships after divorce may be very different from what they were when you were married. You will certainly find your circle of friends shifting after divorce. When you were married, for better or worse, you always had one friend, your spouse, no matter what. For a time, you may actually feel friendless and lonely, but God will provide the friends you need. Some will be old friends you rediscover; some will be brand-new.

You will find yourself making more single friends now, for many of the same reasons you will lose married friends. Your initial compatibility with them may be sharing the pain of divorce, but that will mature into something deeper and more lasting. Spiritual growth; creative and community interests; love of travel, books, and music will eventually replace the attraction of common misery and lead to a shared history that will be separate from your former life.

I hope you will be able to have a few casual friends of the opposite sex. All of us need to guard against the phenomenon of man-hating or woman-hating—lumping the entire opposite sex into the same bucket with our ex-spouses, especially if there was abuse or cruelty involved in the marriage. Of course, we do not want to get involved sexually, but having a few healthy opposite-sex friendships is very healing. We do not need to hate to be safe. We need to be on the lookout for normal men/women and watch how they act, how they treat others. We need an occasional chaste hug from a person of the other gender. We need to have good conversations with them. We need to see the difference between normal and what we experienced, whether we ever choose to get married again or not.

Be prepared for changes in your friendships. Don't be disappointed if you lose old friends; be on the alert for new ones. Strengthen the friendships you've had, especially if you neglected them in the last years of your marriage. And pray for and open yourself to the people God wants in your life.

Facing Your Past

This is a good time to begin a particular task of healing after divorce: facing and healing our pasts. Whatever happened in our marriage that led to divorce, we chose that man or woman as our mate. We had our own motives and issues that led to that choice. And if we do not figure out what those reasons were, there will always be that part of us that is flawed and wounded. We may even marry the same type of person again.

Many of us come out of divorce with our focus on what our ex did. In some cases, much of the fault does lie with one spouse. If our spouse was addicted, abusive, adulterous, or simply indifferent to the marriage, we can make a good case that he or she caused the divorce. But that would hardly be the whole truth of the matter.

Not one of us can walk away from a failed marriage and say, "It was all her or his fault." Life is never that uncomplicated. If this person was so dysfunctional, why did we choose him or her to marry? Remember that we only attract to ourselves someone who is as healed and healthy as we are. So, what was there about this dysfunctional / addicted / cheating / abusive / indifferent person that we fell in love with?

We could say, "I was too young. I didn't know." But, in some sense, we did know. We knew all about her or his defects, and we either thought they were unimportant, or we thought we could change things. Sometimes, we want a certain type of mate because he or she will be easy to control. Our spouse's faults always mirror our own. Our spouse's personality is always, in some way, complementary to ours or fulfills some lack in our life.

If this seems harsh, let me be the first to confess. My husband seemed the ideal mate when I married him two days after my nineteenth birthday. Why? I came from a home dominated by my father's alcohol and drug addictions, an emotional, chaotic, insecure household where we never knew what was going to happen next. My husband, on the other hand, was a very sober, serious, neat, and controlled person with plenty of worldly ambitions and drive. Whether I admitted it to myself then or not, a lot of the attraction was that he would never let me be poor again. "He isn't my father, so he must be OK," was my reasoning.

That is, of course, an oversimplification of our relationship. I believe we could have overcome all that if the commitment had been there, if we had matured normally over the years. Most couples go into marriage pretty clueless and filled with baggage from childhood. Many of us grow out of those perceptions and go on to something more adult. But that was my state of mind when I married. A lot of other stuff went wrong in those thirty years, starting with Vietnam (not just the yearlong separation but the horrors of war), but that's where we started. It wasn't a good beginning. I should have waited until I knew more about life and myself before I married. I had been counseled to do so by wiser people than me. In fact, almost everyone I knew begged me to wait. But I chose to ignore them and went ahead with the wedding.

If I can face my ulterior motives and the reasons behind my decisions, so can you. It's not easy, and it's not going to be pretty when you uncover those dark secrets you've hidden away for so long. But there is freedom and healing in this kind of honesty. Most of all, it takes the focus off your ex and your feelings of victimization, and puts a good kind of power in your own hands. Like forgiveness, facing your own culpability in what went wrong in your marriage is a form of closure.

Facing your past and admitting your fault in the failure of your marriage is part of building a good foundation for the future. It removes something that could undermine your new life. If you do not know what went wrong in your marriage, you will always be handicapped by that ignorance. Once you acknowledge and recover from whatever issues you've hidden deep inside, whatever secret motives were there when you married, you have a better chance of going on to a completely new and happier reality.

For Reflection

1. What kind of progress are you making in being intentional about meeting God daily and on the Sabbath? What do you need to begin or enhance this process? Time? A quiet place? A daily reminder to stop and pray?

_____

_____

_____

_____

_____

2. What differences have you noticed so far in the friendships you experienced while married and your current friendships? Are these changes good? What can you do to make more time for friendships?

_____

_____

_____

_____

_____

3. How do you feel about facing your own culpability in what was wrong in your marriage? What were some of your reasons for marrying the person you married? You may want to explore these issues with a professional counselor or spiritual director.

_____

_____

_____

_____

_____

4. Take some time to write your own thoughts.

_____

_____

_____

_____

_____

_____

_____

_____

_____

_____

_____

_____

_____

_____

_____

_____

_____

_____

_____

_____

_____

_____

_____

_____

_____

_____

_____

_____

_____

chapter thirteen

INVESTING IN
YOUR FUTURE

Life is a decision.... When you believe in a dream, you need
to risk. You could wind up waiting forever if you wait until
everything looks easy.
—Henriette Anne Klauser, PH.D. *Write It Down, Make It
Happen: Knowing What You Want—and Getting It!*[1]

A year after my divorce, I was browsing the writing section of a bookstore. I came across a little book by Henriette Anne Klauser. Turned out,
the book had been in the wrong section of the bookstore. It was not
about the craft of writing at all, but about dreaming and helping those
dreams come true.

Klauser's book was one of the best purchases I could have made then.
She made me think about my future in a whole new way. Story after
story of people who articulated their creative dreams and then made
them happen inspired me to start dreaming. This was a turning point in
my life. I was getting tired of my job as a newspaper reporter (although
I loved my coworkers) and longed to write freelance for the Christian
market. I had never greatly loved the area where I lived; it was my ex-
husband's birthplace and I wasn't on good terms with most of his family at the time. My children were getting ready to graduate from college
and looking for jobs in other parts of the country. And my mother, who
lived in Arizona, had just been widowed.

During a vacation in Arizona, I brought Klauser's book and an empty notebook with me. I read and wrote, wrote and read, trying to set down what I was feeling, that elusive "something" beneath my consciousness that wanted to get out. I had a dream; I just couldn't figure out what it was.

It was only on the flight home a week later that I narrowed my dream down to its essence: "I want to quit my job, move to Arizona, and write full-time." Once I wrote that down, I knew it to be the truth. How I would do that, I did not know. But I felt God smiling at me, I felt my heart lift, I had direction.

I started telling people, at first very tentatively. What would my children think about my selling their childhood home and moving two thousand miles away? I was to be surprised. "Oh, Mom, that would be so cool. You should do it!" was their reaction. My psychologist was probably the most enthusiastic. "This is the first time I've heard you talk about investing in the future," he said. My mother, of course, was ecstatic; I couldn't get out there fast enough for her.

Moving two thousand miles away was easy compared to the career move I planned. I had no idea how I would get a freelance writing career started. I had a book idea that seemed pretty good to me. I planned to take six months off to explore it before looking for a part-time job to support myself. As it turned out, I never got that job. Four months after moving to Arizona, I attended a Catholic Writers Retreat in nearby Tucson. After making the necessary connections and much hard work, I had a contract for my first book: *Make Room for God: Clearing Out the Clutter*. (I had learned a lot about inner clutter from the divorce and outer clutter from the cross-country move).

That is the bare bones of my story. It leaves out all the doubts, fears, and delays; the fourteen months it took to sell my old house; the miracle of finding my new home right at the base of a mountain I had loved and visited for thirty years. The first night I spent in my new life in Arizona the full moon rose over the mountain exactly as I had seen it in a dream. That made it all worthwhile. The dream had finally come true. I was home at last.

Discovering Your Dreams

How can you discover and then encourage your hidden dreams? You'll have to start as I did, with little but an empty notebook and a good pen. Start writing. Start exploring your inner landscape for clues. What did you love doing as a child that you gave up in adulthood because it was impractical or you were told you couldn't make a living doing that? What interests have you put off because you never had the time or because your marriage sapped all your energy? How do you really feel about your job, your hometown, your education, your life in general? Is there any geographic area you feel drawn to? Are there changes you would like to make? And what intersection of all these factors might pinpoint your deepest and fondest dream in one simple sentence?

Give yourself lots of time to discover your dreams. As a survivor of divorce, you've taken a beating to your self-esteem and even your ability to dream. The exploration of your dreams is healing in itself. You don't need to know it all or even as clearly as I did. You just need to discover yourself again. You need to get acquainted with you.

Answering the Question, "Who Are you?" Is the Key

Unlocking your dreams and knowing who you are as a person are two sides to the same question. Your interests and gifts show who you are; and who you are is the key to knowing what you should be doing with your life in this world.

After decades of being someone's wife, of raising three children, of jobs, church and community volunteering, then college late in life, I usually defined myself by what I did. The question of who I was never occurred to me until I started talking to a wonderful spiritual director. "You're a human being, not a human doing," he reminded me—many times.

So, I took the question, "Who am I?" to God, who seemed eminently qualified to give an answer. And I got a response rather quickly: "You are mine."

Now, that's pretty cool! After a failed marriage, it's good to know you belong to someone who loves you and cherishes you. I hadn't felt loved or cherished for a long time.

God's "you are mine" is not the same as what a sinful human being (especially in a bad marriage) might mean by those words. It doesn't mean, "You are mine to treat however I see fit, to use, to vent my anger on, to ignore."

God's "you are mine" is full of possibility, potential, and promise. God's "you are mine" means, "You are my creation; free to become who you choose to become."

So, explore your potential. There's something very beautiful inside you that longs to get out, some creative dream that has been incubating for a long, long time. Let it come into the light. Where will it lead? Only God knows, but I suspect it will lead to a great adventure and, eventually, to the very gates of heaven.

For Reflection

1. Write God a letter pouring out all your feelings, hopes, and dreams about the kind of life you would like to have. Answer this question: If I were not afraid and money were not an issue, what would I do with the rest of my life?

_____

_____

_____

_____

_____

_____

_____

_____

2. If you have already come up with a specific dream, write it on index cards and place them all over your house where you will see them daily. With whom can you share your dream and find encouragement?

_____

_____

_____

_____

_____

3. What challenges are you experiencing in making your dream happen? Are there fears that are holding you back? What small, concrete actions might you take right now to make your dream happen?

_____

_____

_____

_____

_____

4. Take some time to write your own thoughts.

_____

_____

_____

_____

_____

_____

_____

_____

_____

_____

_____

_____

part four

THE

REST

OF

THE

JOURNEY

Do not remember the former things,
or consider the things of old.
I am about to do a new thing;
now it springs forth,
do you not perceive it?
—Isaiah 43:18–19

chapter fourteen

TRUSTING IN LOVE

I will trust, and will not be afraid, for the Lord God
is my strength and my might;
he has become my salvation.
—Isaiah 12:2

Trust in the Lord with all your heart; and do not
rely on your own insight.
—Proverbs 3:5

On the rest of our journey through this life, there are some important skills we need to learn, skills we may not have had the chance to learn during marriage. We need to leave behind some of our old baggage and travel lightly with new attitudes and beliefs, with a simpler way of being. Part Four is about all these things: Learning to trust God, developing new beliefs and a new attitude about our finances, and balancing the demands of this world and our relationship with God.

Learning to trust God is one of the more difficult tasks of growing in our spiritual lives. It may be especially hard for us who are divorced. We have experienced disillusionment and failure in our relationships. How do we learn to trust the God we cannot see when the people in our lives, whom we can see, have let us down?

The Object of Our Trust Must Be Trustworthy

If we are to trust anyone—God, other human beings, or ourselves—the object of our confidence must be worthy of trust. Ultimately, we can only trust another to be who they are. We cannot trust in our expectations or our dreams about one another. We cannot practice wishful thinking and denial, then be shocked and surprised when someone proves not to be trustworthy. We learned this the hard way in our marriages.

Human beings are wonderful creations of God, but because of our sinfulness, we are also flawed, clueless, and self-centered. We are works in progress, certainly not perfect. Because of that, no one we meet on this planet can be entirely trusted, even the person we see in the mirror. Only God can be trusted. And that is the key. If we can only trust another to be what he or she is, then God, being entirely holy and perfect, is entirely trustworthy.

The word *entrust* means "to assign the care of something to someone." Who is worthy to be assigned the care of our souls, our very selves? Whom do we trust with our deepest hopes, hurts, and fears? Who can heal us? Our efforts to put that kind of trust in other human beings has failed. We may decide "the only one I can trust is me." But we find even we are not all that trustworthy.

But God is not like us. God is not subject to the weakness and instability of normal human interactions. We are flawed. God is not. We are incomplete. God is not. We are clueless. God is not. God has no issues, no difficulty being available, no lack of love, no bad days. God is completely whole and free and is in no need of healing or enlightenment.

We have let our perception of God be tainted by our own failures and our disappointment with other people. And we have blamed God for our own errors and misjudgments. When we understand that God is not like us, that God is not a flawed human being, trusting God is not quite so difficult.

God's Ways and Human Ways

Often, our reluctance to trust God is because God's ways are often radically different from human methods. Sometimes we feel this is a good thing. For example, Scripture assures us that in God's kingdom, the rich and mighty are displaced from their positions of power, while the poor, the hungry, the sorrowful, and the persecuted are given a special place (see Luke 1:46–55 and 6:20–49). For those of us who have felt powerless and victimized by the mighty and those of us who have experienced poverty, illness, and ridicule, God's ways can seem fair and just.

But there are plenty of times when we just don't like God's methods, especially where our interests are concerned. For one thing, God moves a lot more slowly than we would, if we were in charge. And, as Christians, we are not allowed to just let it rip, to say and do whatever our emotions tell us, when we are faced with conflict or people who are acting ugly, whether these people are our ex-spouses, our children, our coworkers, or the driver in the next car on the highway.

God's ways are not our ways, nor are God's thoughts our thoughts (see Isaiah 55:8). God's ways do not make sense by our human logic. This can make trusting God somewhat difficult, until we remember that God is entirely trustworthy and perfect.

But...What If...?

There is another reason we find trusting God difficult. Let's be honest and admit that much of our distrust comes from wanting to control our own lives.

My favorite excuse when I choose not to trust God is the "what if?" argument. What if God doesn't come through for me? What if the worst happens (whatever that is)? What if trusting God doesn't work? What if I'm really on my own in this situation? Ultimately, our trust in God depends on our being able to silence that fearful inner voice.

Oftentimes, we are not very worried about God being trustworthy. We are more worried that God's solution to our problems will not be to our liking. The big "what if" is "What if I don't like what happens if I turn this situation over to God?" Behind every act of self-reliance, every doubt about God's trustworthiness, lurks our own sin, which says, "I can do this better myself. I don't want to give up control. God won't do it the way I want it done."

We can choose to trust God. We can also choose to manage our own lives, to do what we think is best, according to our own lights. We will learn to trust God when we are ready to surrender, to admit the results of trusting ourselves haven't been satisfactory.

How Do We Begin to Trust God?

We learn to trust God the way we learn any new skill. We do it a little bit at a time. We try and fail, and we try again. God will offer opportunities to trust as we move on to our new lives after divorce. We will begin to see God coming through, providing our needs, giving us good friends, showing us where to go. If we are observant, if we give God the credit, we will see how trustworthy God is.

Ultimately, we learn to trust God by spending time with God. The more we spend time with anyone, the more we get to know them. In the same way, our trust in God will grow in direct proportion to our knowledge of God.

While I cannot claim complete and total trust in God today, I have seen much progress in the years since my divorce. Most of time, I live in a state of trust. I've stopped feeling that it's all up to me. I was once the sole director of my life; it has been a relief to relinquish that role. It has been wonderful to find Someone who is worthy of my trust and confidence.

Trust means relinquishing control—over our lives, our circumstances, our time. We do not need to micromanage life; we simply need to live it. Trusting God is a very practical arrangement, and it leaves us freer, calmer, and happier.

For Reflection

1. Do you find it difficult to trust God because of your disappointment in other people, especially your ex-spouse?

_____

_____

_____

_____

_____

2. On a scale of 1 through 10, rate your trust in God, with 1 meaning "I don't trust God at all" and 10 being "I trust God freely, like the birds of the air." Then write about why you rated your trust that way.

_____

_____

_____

_____

_____

3. What answers to prayer do you need today? Are you willing to see how God answers them, or are you anxious that God answer them precisely as you want?

_____

_____

_____

_____

_____

4. Take some time to write your own thoughts.

_____

_____

_____

_____

chapter fifteen

FACING FINANCIAL REALITIES

For where your treasure is,
there your heart will be also.
—Luke 12:34

I would like to have enough money so I'd never have to worry about money again.

Until recently, that was my mantra anytime I paid bills. Since I began this new life of mine—quitting my job, moving to Arizona, and dedicating myself to freelance writing—my biggest worry has been finances. Even though I am happily single and mostly content with life these days, looking at my checkbook can stir deep feelings of insecurity. I have experienced much success in my writing, more than I ever dreamed. But my cash-challenged status can make me forget just how good God has been to me.

If you are divorced, your financial situation has almost certainly worsened. It may be the chief topic of your prayers these days. It was probably a shock when the realities of dissolving your marriage dawned on you.

Let's look at that statement in the first line of this chapter. How much money would any of us need to never have to worry about money ever again? Married or divorced, rich or poor, successful or not, that's a pretty nebulous goal.

Jesus said we are not to worry. It is one of his best and best-known pieces of advice:

> Therefore I tell you, do not worry about your life, what you will eat or what you will drink, or about your body, what you will wear. Is not life more than food, and the body more than clothing? Look at the birds of the air; they neither sow nor reap nor gather into barns, and yet your heavenly Father feeds them. Are you not of more value than they? And can any of you by worrying add a single hour to your span of life?... For it is the Gentiles who strive for all these things; and indeed your heavenly Father knows that you need all these things. But strive first for the kingdom of God and his righteousness, and all these things will be given to you as well. (Matthew 6:25–33)

The logic of Jesus' words is the promise in the last sentence. If we will concentrate on the kingdom, on developing our relationships with God and one another, God takes care of the rest. Our human logic argues, "Shouldn't we take care of the little stuff and God take care of the big stuff?" No, Jesus says. Seek the kingdom first, and let God take care of the basics.

For those of us who are divorced, trusting our finances to God is difficult. Few of us do well financially after a divorce. There are exceptions. But for the vast majority of us, divorce is anywhere from distressing to financially ruinous. The reason is simple: If you take any household, all living under the same roof, sharing food, electricity, expenses, and then separate them into two households with the same income, they will not be as well off. This is reality, simple math. Many people today are overextended on credit cards, upside down on mortgages, unemployed, underemployed, or bankrupt. Divorce only makes matters worse financially.

These days, as happy as I normally am to be single, I still have moments of deep insecurity and fear. It's difficult to pay all the bills and find there is little money left for food and incidentals. It's frustrating when there's nothing extra for an unexpected house or car repair. I can't help my children out very much when they are struggling. An inexpensive vacation means going into more debt, which takes months to pay off.

That does not change Jesus' words: "Don't worry."

I never thought much about finances when I was married. My husband made a good salary. I stayed home with the children until they were all in school. Then I started a little home business. I didn't have to worry about how successful it was. I had that financial security of my husband's income. We lived simply, paid off our mortgage early, saved for three college educations, put away for retirement. Our children could take music and karate lessons. We took vacations each year. Life was easy then. There was enough money coming in that the regular bills were no problem and an unexpected medical bill or auto repair was no problem. To me, that was financial security.

Those days are over. I suspect they are over for a good many of us, divorced or not. Things change—that is the only sure thing in this life. Getting angry or feeling guilty is a bad use of energy. How much energy do any of us have to spare these days?

When you are tempted to feel sorry for yourself or angry with your ex-spouse, remember the other side of the equation. Why did you get a divorce? What was going on? In my case, the finances were fine, but I lived in misery, fought depression constantly, and felt unloved, guilty, sad, and inadequate for years—decades. When the marriage fell apart, it was a release into a whole new life for me, a life of healing, accomplishment, and rediscovering my true self.

If God had come to me and told me my future, this future that I live today, I would not have changed my choices. And it still looks like a good deal to me, even when I can't balance my checkbook. Would I still trade my former financial security with all the problems of my marriage for freedom, self-esteem, the love of friends and family, and work that I love? The answer is always yes, every time.

Gratitude is the key to managing our finances after divorce. If we remember where we have been and where we are now, we will be grateful. Our welfare and security are God's responsibility. Our responsibilities are so much easier: Get up in the morning, spend time with God, do what we can each day, play and have fun every day, and trust that God will take care of the rest. God is my security now, financial and otherwise.

God's care is a daily thing. "Give us this day our daily bread," Jesus taught us to pray. What that means is that none of us, especially we who are divorced, can look too far ahead. We must look instead to our immediate needs—and bring them before the Lord with trust and expectancy. "Lord, I need fifty dollars to pay that electric bill," is sure to be answered. "Lord, I just wish you'd let me win the lottery; I can handle it!" will not!

It isn't that God does not trust us with large sums of money (pause for laughter).

God has other goals in mind for us than the small and unworthy goals we make for ourselves. God's goal for each of us is that we will become the people God created us to be: sons and daughters of the Most High, the great creator of the universe. How's that for a huge goal?

We won't get there by being independent of God in any area of life. We get there by being in relationship with God—a daily, close, intimate union.

When I ask God for that big windfall that will make me financially secure, I'm asking God to be sure I don't have to depend on anyone but myself.

Lately, I've been cultivating a new attitude when it comes to financial security. I've stopped muttering to myself (as I pay bills), "I wish I had enough money so I'd never have to worry about money again." I am learning, in gratitude and trust, to say, "God is taking care of me today. I will always have enough. I don't need to worry about money." And, so, my prayer has been answered!

For Reflection

1. Since your divorce, how have your finances been? Better? Worse? The same? Are you finding it harder or easier to take care of your finances since your divorce? Why is that?

_____

_____

_____

_____

_____

2. What was your role in managing the finances in your marriage? What is your role now, as a single person?

_____

_____

_____

_____

_____

3. Take some time to write your own thoughts.

_____

_____

_____

_____

_____

_____

_____

_____

_____

chapter sixteen

DEVELOPING NEW
PARADIGMS

...you will know the truth, and the truth will make you free.
—John 8:32

Divorce has a way of shattering our old paradigms, perceptions, and beliefs. We have had to overhaul what we were taught, examine what we accepted without question, toss out our favorite clichés. God, as it turns out, is not who we thought. We are divorced, but we find ourselves still loved by God and loved more tenderly than ever. Many of us are beginning to heal from the whole experience, are discovering hope, happiness, and a spiritual freedom we never knew before.

Since my divorce, God has been showing me my old prejudices, beliefs, and assumptions. Giving up these tired, worn paradigms in favor of new beliefs has helped free me from the emotional and spiritual baggage I have been carrying all my life. While I cannot know what your pet paradigms are, here are a few of my own. Perhaps they will sound familiar to you.

"There's a Right Way and a Wrong Way to Do Everything!"
Growing up, I heard this phrase from a lot of adults, and came to believe it absolutely, if unconsciously. Trouble was, no one bothered to explain exactly what the "right" way was, and I never asked. Life became one long quest to find the Right Way. Even as an adult, I was on this quest.

What did everyone else know, for instance, about housekeeping that I was missing? I did a lot of reading on the right way to clean house. Heloise and Don Aslett were my heroes; *The Messies Manual* my second favorite book after the Bible. Even so, my house was always a mess. I kept searching. There had to be an answer, a Right Way. I just had to find it.

When God brought this belief to my consciousness, it sounded silly. Yet, it explained a lot about my attempts to find a solution to every problem and situation. It also explained my reluctance to start any new project, especially a big writing project. Had I discovered the Right Way to do this? Or was I going to go down the wrong path and have to start all over? Since giving up this idea about the Right Way, I have found my decisions and my daily life much easier. Knowing the truth has, indeed, set me free.

"If Anything Has Gone Wrong, It Must Be My Fault"

No one ever told me this; it was something I internalized as a child living in an alcoholic, dysfunctional family. It is common in children of alcoholic parents, but children can develop this belief in any stressful family situation. Perhaps it starts as wishful thinking, then graduates to "if I could only do something." Finally, we subconsciously assume "it must be my fault." Self-blame is an idea that creeps in there quietly and furtively, a tool that our soul's enemy uses to keep us in a state of guilt and shame all our lives.

The belief that we are somehow, and always, at fault is a very effective way to block God's love for us. Scrupulosity, perfectionism, self-hatred, and depression can all result from this assumption. In John's Gospel, chapter four, Jesus spoke of "living water" flowing from within us. The belief that it's all our fault acts as a huge dam blocking that flow. It will cripple us over and over again, every time we begin to draw closer to God.

Perhaps this core belief has crept into your thinking over the years. It may have been part of your marriage. Maybe your ex-spouse laid this one on you. There is nothing like pushing the blame on another to avoid facing the truth about ourselves. Many of us have the type of personality and background that we take all the blame for everything upon ourselves. We need to let this paradigm go. We should accept responsibility for our own choices and actions, and that is all. We cannot take on the emotions, decisions, and lifestyles of other people, even those closest to us.

I suspect that believing everything is our fault is an attempt to control people and things. If we believe that, we may also believe that we can affect situations and save people. When we give up that belief, we find our lives moving more smoothly. We can concentrate on our own lives and on the present moment and leave the rest in God's hands.

Childish Beliefs About God and Prayer

So far, I have written about paradigms we picked up in childhood through no fault of our own. But the ultimate childish paradigm is one many of us hold about God. It is a perception of God as magician. We treat God as someone who should do things for us—then leave us alone. It has nothing to do with a real relationship with the Creator.

The great Christian author and apologist C.S. Lewis freely admits this was his image of God as an eight-year-old child whose mother was dying of cancer.

> I had approached God, or my idea of God, without love, without awe, even without fear. He was, in my mental picture of this miracle, to appear neither as Savior nor as Judge, but merely as a magician; and when He had done what was required of Him I supposed He would simply—well, go away. It never crossed my mind that the tremendous contact which I solicited should have any consequences beyond restoring the *status quo.*[1]

Lewis believed that an image of God as magician is quite normal and does no harm in a little child. After all, belief in wishes, fairy tales, and Santa

Claus are part of childhood. But our image of and relationship with God is supposed to mature. As Saint Paul writes, "When I was a child, I spoke like a child, I thought like a child, I reasoned like a child; when I became an adult, I put an end to childish ways" (1 Corinthians 13:11).

There are many of us whose Christian walk has stayed in the baby or toddler stage all our lives. There are churches that encourage this; it makes controlling the members easier. Still, we have no one but ourselves to blame. We have not wanted a mature walk with God; we have been content to drift along, carried along passively, expecting that our light commitment is enough for eternal glory. Then our marriages collapsed and our lives were shattered. What that must have done to our childish beliefs in God, especially when our prayers for help seemed to go unanswered! It is time to rethink our paradigms about God. We can no longer stay in the baby stage of Christianity; it just does not work.

My relationship with God has matured over the years since I fully committed my life to Jesus at the age of nineteen. Yet, I have found this image of God as magician lurking down there, in the depths of my heart. Go back to chapter one in this book and my prayer: "How could you?" That's immaturity. That's unreality. That's gross misunderstanding of who God is and what God does. I have gone beyond that now; divorce did that for me. And I find my relationship with God is much healthier and happier these days.

There are all kinds of old, false beliefs and perceptions operating in our hearts. They hide in the darkness in the recesses of our minds, leaping at any opportunity to interrupt and incapacitate us, just when we were making progress, becoming happier and healthier, getting closer to God. Ultimately, only God knows about all of them and knows how to get rid of them.

Give God permission to turn the lights on inside and show you the false beliefs hiding in the dark inside. Be willing to give them up and replace them with healthy, realistic perceptions. Remember Jesus' promise to us that we will know the truth and the truth will make us free.

For Reflection

1. Have you been told throughout life that there is a right way and a wrong way to do everything? Have you internalized that belief?

_____

_____

_____

_____

_____

2. Do you often blame yourself when things go wrong? When did that belief start? In childhood? In your marriage?

_____

_____

_____

_____

_____

3. Do you have a childish image of God as magician? How do you know? How do you sometimes pray that proves this is part of your belief system?

_____

_____

_____

_____

_____

4. Take some time to write your own thoughts.

_____

_____

_____

_____

_____

chapter seventeen

FINDING YOUR BALANCE

Peace I leave with you; my peace I give to you.
I do not give to you as the world gives.
—John 14:27

Spiritual balance is basic to our well-being. In this world, it is difficult to find that balance, especially after the pain and suffering of divorce. If that weren't enough, our spiritual equilibrium is constantly threatened by our culture's insistence on self-reliance, productivity, individualism, and consumerism. There is little room for God in a life that is filled with endless activities from morning to night, yet that is what our culture demands and expects.

It is important that we who have experienced divorce find our spiritual balance now. It may have been many years since we have felt stable and at peace. When our marital relationships were failing, many of us threw ourselves into trying to save our marriages. Or we may have immersed ourselves in a career, projects, or volunteerism to avoid confronting our problems. The divorce process kept us busy. When was the last time we felt balanced or took a break from the drama and emotions of the divorce and of everyday life?

What Is Spiritual Balance?
Spiritual balance means that God's peace, which Jesus promised us, is the fundamental orientation of our lives. Worrying about things instead

of surrendering them to God will upset our balance. So will rushing around, trying to do too much, neglecting to take time for prayer and silence.

Spiritual balance means we do not let the world and its systems dictate to us how we should feel, what we should think, how much we should get done. Spiritual balance means we remember who we are in Jesus Christ, that we are destined for eternity, not slaves of this world.

Spiritual balance means discerning when it is time to act and when it is time to let God act. Ordinarily, we don't give much thought to this. Many of our actions are automatic. We get up at a certain time, wash ourselves, prepare our meals, drive our cars, and do our jobs on autopilot much of the time.

But all of life cannot be lived on autopilot. Not if we call ourselves Christians. There are constant intersections in life where we must decide what course to take. What do we do when we are angry and see a confrontation approaching? What if we need to make better choices about our lifestyle and diet? How do we make choices about our relationships, our careers, our dreams? What if we realize our commitment to God and to our loved ones is lacking? As Christians, we cannot be passive and do whatever is comfortable and non-threatening. Nor can we take every situation upon ourselves as our sole responsibility, believing that our own efforts and willpower are all that is needed.

In order to stay spiritually balanced, we cannot be in control at all times. We can make ourselves crazy thinking we have to do everything in our power, or we will miss opportunities or God's will. We belong to God, so we need have no such worries. God does not play games with us or expect us to guess what his will is. If we are missing something, if we have forgotten something important, if we should be doing something, God will bring us back to it again. We can trust God to be very involved and interested in our lives.

For our part, we must stay in touch with God at all times. We need to keep communicating, which is all that prayer is. We need to discuss all our situations and decisions with God. We should feel free to ask God any question, no matter how mundane, and we should trust that God will answer us.

There is another way we Christians can get out of balance. That is when we are so busy doing God's work that we neglect our relationship with God. Almost a hundred years ago, Oswald Chambers warned young men preparing for the mission field to avoid this pitfall. "The measure of the worth of our public activity for God is the private profound communion we have with Him," Chambers said. "Rush is wrong every time, there is always plenty of time to worship God."[1]

The Sabbath Helps Our Balance

The commandment to keep the Sabbath every week was not intended to add an arbitrary rule to our lives. The Sabbath mandate is actually the one commandment that addresses how we treat ourselves. The first few Commandments have to do with our relationship to God; the last our relationships with other people. But the Sabbath commandment is for us. It is God's antidote to our culture's insistence on endless work, productivity, and activity. The Sabbath means we have God's permission to walk away from it all one day a week.

Ignoring the Sabbath, doing work, chores, and activities seven days a week, will quickly pull us out of spiritual balance and into chaos and confusion. Insisting on that one day to be quiet, to do nothing productive, to regroup, will bring us back to that "peace of God, which surpasses all understanding" (Philippians 4:7).

Floating as a Metaphor for Balance

Finding our spiritual balance in this life is a lot like floating in water. Although it looks completely passive, floating takes attention and constant adjustment. One cannot be passive and continue to float. The back must be arched just so to keep the face out of the water. Minute movements of trunk, arms, and legs must be made to keep the body up. Floating is relaxing, but one cannot fall asleep; the human body does not float like a cork on top of the water. Left to its own devices, the heaviest parts of the human body will sink just enough to make breathing impossible. That is why people who lose consciousness in the water drown.

Floating is a wonderful metaphor for the spiritual life. God does not mean for us to be limp and passive, destined to be swept along by whatever currents life brings. On the other hand, we are not to be in complete control, like a long-distance swimmer who makes no progress without continuous effort. When we try to control our lives like that, we end up exhausted. Floating is the perfect image of the spiritual life. It combines a patient trust in the one who determines where the currents of life will lead, with an active attention to keeping ourselves in the center of God's will, in other words, to keeping afloat.

Ultimately, spiritual balance, like physical balance, becomes a natural thing. We do not think about our balance while we are walking or doing other physical activities—unless we lose our balance. Then we pay attention to it. In the same way, our spiritual balance will become natural, something we do not think about unless it is absent.

If we want to develop good spiritual balance, we must be intentional about it. We must intentionally slow down, quiet down, and remember who we are.

For Reflection

1. How has your divorce upset your sense of spiritual balance?

_____

_____

_____

_____

_____

_____

2. Do you tend to try to do too much, to control life when you are out of balance? Or do you tend to be too passive, to give up, when things are going badly?

_____

_____

_____

_____

_____

3. Are you a swimmer or at least able to float? If so, describe what floating feels like to you. Do you find floating scary or pleasant?

_____

_____

_____

_____

4. Take some time to write your own thoughts.

_____

_____

_____

_____

_____

_____

_____

_____

_____

chapter eighteen

LEARNING TO FLY

A bird's not defined by being grounded but by his ability to
fly. Remember this, humans are not defined by their limita-
tions, but by the intentions I have for them;
not by what they seem to be, but by everything it means to
be created in my image.
—William Paul Young, *The Shack*[1]

You are a gift. You have always been a gift, to God and to everyone around you. More than likely, you have never known that. Certainly, during your marriage, you weren't treated as a gift. But that does not change reality. God made you, and you are unique and special. No one is like you. No one else has your personality, your combination of gifts, your special way of living and of seeing life.

There is joy and contentment in your future. If you are too soon out of the woods of your divorce and cannot see it yet, you need to believe you have a bright future. Things do get better. You will find that your divorce has freed you in ways you cannot imagine now. You will be free in new ways to become your true self, to grow, to love and be loved.

One of the skills I have learned since my divorce is the knack of staying in the present moment. The past became too painful to wallow in, and there was nothing I could do about it. The future looked uncertain; I could not predict what might happen. All I could do was stay in the here-and-now moment. I found there was plenty to do in the present moment. I had classes, I had work, I had books and music and a dog to keep me company. And, most of all, I had God, who is always and forever in the eternal present. When I learned to stay put, to stop letting my imagination travel back to the past or forward to the future, I found contentment and calm. I also found reality. And I found that I was able to go on, make good decisions, cope with the pain, and emerge into God's joy.

"I don't know what's going to happen now," you might be saying to yourself. Many of us feel the same way after a divorce has shaken us to the core. We don't know what is going to happen, and we are afraid of the future. What we must remember is that we never did know what was going to happen. We assumed we did. We thought everything would go on as it had, comfortably and predictably. But the unexpected is a normal part of this life. Uncertainty has always been the reality, whether we admitted it or not.

Uncertainty is not a bad thing, although it seems so if we are overly concerned with safety and security. Author Oswald Chambers viewed staying calm in uncertainty as a good and spiritual trait that Christians should cultivate:

> ...gracious uncertainty is the mark of the spiritual life. To be certain of God means that we are uncertain in all our ways, we do not know what a day may bring forth. This is generally said with a sigh of sadness, it should be rather an expression of breathless expectation. We are uncertain of the next step, but we are certain of God. Immediately, we abandon to God and do the duty that lies nearest, He packs our life with surprises all the time.... Leave the whole thing to him, it is gloriously uncertain how He will come in, but He will come.[2]

"Breathless expectation" and a life packed with surprises. Those words put a new perspective on the uncertainties of life, especially life after divorce. We are not always comfortable with that. But God loves to surprise us and wants us to trust and be willing to live in God's glorious uncertainty.

Flying Lessons

Many of us know the song, "On Eagle's Wings." Recently, I heard a talk by Father Paul Coutinho, a Jesuit priest from India, in which he warned his audience to be careful what they ask for when they sing that song. He told this story to illustrate his point: When it is time for a baby eaglet to learn to fly, its mother carries it high in the sky…and dumps the baby off its back. The eaglet screams and struggles as it begins to plummet toward the earth. Over and over, the mother eagle swoops below the baby, catches it, and carries it up again. Finally, the baby learns. It spreads its wings…and makes the sky its home. Flying lessons may be terrifying, but the end result is a creature who can now do what it was meant to do.

You, too, were meant for something higher and greater than the life you have been living. Like those baby eagles, you must be willing to let your heavenly Father lift you higher and teach you to fly. Unlike the eagles, though, you do not belong only to the sky. You belong to eternity.

For Reflection

1. Now that your clipped wings are on the mend—as is your broken heart—how do you feel? Are you hopeful? Take some time to think and write about it—before taking flight!

_____

_____

_____

_____

_____

_____

appendix

THE ANNULMENT PROCESS
OF THE CATHOLIC CHURCH

For those readers who are members of the Catholic church, there is an annulment process which divorced members must go through before they can remarry. This section will address some of that procedure, but your best source of information will be your own pastor and/or diocesan tribunal, which is the office which handles annulments.

First, let's dispel some of the myths about Catholics and divorce. A Catholic declaration of nullity (the technical term for the layperson's term *annulment*) is not "Catholic divorce," nor does it say the marriage never took place. It does not make the children of the marriage illegitimate. Your divorce did not make your children illegitimate; Catholic annulment does not, either. Another myth about Catholicism and divorce is that the divorced cannot receive any of the sacraments. This is not true. As a divorcee, your status in the church is not changed; you still receive Communion and reconciliation as you always have; you can still receive the anointing of the sick when and if you need it. You cannot, however, get married again in the Catholic church unless you go through the annulment process (unless your former spouse dies in the interim).

Because the Catholic church takes marriage so seriously, it reserves the right to regulate who may get married in a Catholic church. A Catholic annulment tribunal of three judges (all of them canon lawyers) makes a decision about the sacramentality of your former marriage, not its legal authenticity. As you have read in chapter two, Christian churches, including the Catholic church, see marriage as a sacred covenant. This covenant cannot be set aside in a civil, legal divorce process and another marriage entered into in a Catholic church. Most churches have some regulations about counseling, classes, or other procedures before remarriage after divorce. The Catholic church's procedure includes the annulment process. If you read carefully my warnings about new relationships after divorce, you can understand the church's reluctance to "rubber stamp" a civil court's divorce decree and allow you to go through the same thing all over again.

Going through the annulment process can be a very healing experience. You will have opportunities to write about what happened in your marriage. The time an annulment usually takes (eighteen months or more) will give you time to get your balance and recover from the trauma you have been through. You will, in effect, get that hearing you may have badly wanted when you were going through the civil divorce.

What does a tribunal look for when they read the testimony of a divorced Catholic? They look for signs that the parties were not prepared for and not ready to enter into a permanent, sacramental covenant marriage with one another. They look for signs that you did not or could not enter into your marriage "freely and without reservation." That is why your tribunal will ask for additional testimony from those who have known you and your ex-spouse for a long time. Parents, siblings, and others who have known you since the beginning of the marriage are your best witnesses. That is why you should begin the annulment process soon after your final divorce decree is granted. People die; friends move away and lose touch; memories fade. Do not wait just because you think you will never marry again. You may meet that man or woman of your dreams years from now. You do not want to make it impossible to get married in your own church because you forgot about or distrusted the Catholic annulment process.

Catholic annulment is actually a very good and healing thing to go through. You will not find it offensive or degrading. I worked for the diocese of Youngstown, Ohio, for seven years and was divorced and went through annulment during that time. I found the tribunal staff to be not only sympathetic and kind, but cheerful and hopeful. They hear all kinds of stories of failed love and trauma. They know how to listen and how to give comfort. To them, helping Catholics get annulments and heal from their divorces is a ministry, not a job.

notes

Chapter One
1. Barbara Leahy Shlemon, *Healing the Wounds of Divorce: A Spiritual Guide to Recovery* (Notre Dame, Ind.: Ave Maria, 1992), p. 19.
2. Shlemon, p. 19.

Chapter Two
1. Seán Wales, C.SS.R. *Catholics and Divorce: Finding Help and Healing Within the Church* (Liguori, Mo.: Liguori, 2005), p. 14.
2. *Catechism of the Catholic Church* (Washington, D.C.: USCCB, 1994), #1609.
3. *CCC*, #1606.

Chapter Three
1. Rowland Croucher, from the Retrouvaille website at http://www.retrouvaille.org, 1995.
2. Visit the Retrouvaille website at http://www.retrouvaille.org/ for more information.

Chapter Four
1. Andrew M. Greeley, *When Life Hurts: Healing Themes From the Gospels* (Chicago: Thomas More, 1988), p. 12.

Chapter Five
1. Catherine Marshall, *Adventures in Prayer* (New York: Ballantine, 1975), p. 19.

Chapter Six
1. Pope John Paul II. World Youth Day, Toronto, Canada, 2002.

Chapter Eight
1. Anne Lamott, *Traveling Mercies: Some Thoughts on Faith* (New York: Anchor, 1999), p. 68.

Chapter Nine
1. Wales, p. 15.
2. William Paul Young, *The Shack* (Los Angeles: Windblown Media, 2007), p. 97.

Chapter Ten
1. Kenneth Atchity, *A Writer's Time: A Guide to the Creative Process from Vision through Revision* (New York. Norton, 1986), p. xvi.

Chapter Eleven
1. Susan K. Rowland, *Make Room for God: Clearing Out the Clutter* (Cincinnati: St. Anthony Messenger Press, 2007), pp. 82–83.

Chapter Twelve
1. Shlemon, p. 81.

Chapter Thirteen
1. Henriette Anne Klauser, PH.D., *Write It Down, Make It Happen: Knowing What You Want— and Getting It!* (New York: Fireside, 2000), pp. 83–84.

Chapter Sixteen
1. C.S. Lewis, *The Inspirational Writings of C.S. Lewis: Surprised by Joy, Reflections on the Psalms, The Four Loves, The Business of Heaven* (New York: Harcourt, Brace and Company, 1994), p. 13.

Chapter Seventeen
1. Oswald Chambers, *My Utmost For His Highest: Selections for the Year* (New York: Dodd, Mead, and Company, 1935), p. 6.

Chapter Eighteen
1. Young, p. 100.
2. Chambers, p. 120.

bibliography

Atchity, Kenneth. *A Writer's Time: A Guide to the Creative Process from Vision through Revision*. New York: Norton, 1986.

Catechism of the Catholic Church. Washington, D.C.: USCCB, 1994.

Chambers, Oswald. *My Utmost For His Highest: Selections for the Year.* New York: Dodd, Mead, and Company, 1935.

Gaede, Stan D. *An Incomplete Guide to the Rest of Your Life*. Downers Grove, Ill.: InterVarsity, 2002.

Greeley, Andrew M. *When Life Hurts: Healing Themes From the Gospels*. Chicago: Thomas More, 1988.

Greteman, James and Leon Haverkamp (revised by Elsie P. Radtke). *Divorce and Beyond: A Workbook for Recovery and Healing*. Skokie, Ill.: ACTA, 1983, 2004.

Klauser, Henriette Anne, PH.D. *Write It Down, Make It Happen: Knowing What You Want—and Getting It!* New York: Fireside, 2000.

Lamott, Anne. *Traveling Mercies: Some Thoughts on Faith*. New York: Anchor, 1999.

Lewis, C.S. *Surprised By Joy*. Copyright 1986, 1984 by Arthur Owen Barfield. Published in *The Inspirational Writings of C.S. Lewis*. New York: Harcourt, Brace and Company, 1994.

Marshall, Catherine. *Adventures in Prayer*. New York: Ballantine, 1975.

Shlemon, Barbara Leahy. *Healing the Wounds of Divorce: A Spiritual Guide to Recovery*. Notre Dame, Ind.: Ave Maria, 1992.

Wales, Seán, C.SS.R. *Catholics and Divorce: Finding Help and Healing Within the Church*. Liguori, Mo.: Liguori, 2005.